IT HAPPENED IN
MASSACHUSETTS

By Larry B. Pletcher

Illustrated by Lisa Harvey

TWODOT
Helena, Montana

A · TWODOT · BOOK

Falcon® is continually expanding its list of regional history books. You can order extra copies of this book and get information and prices for other Falcon® books by writing to Falcon®, P.O. Box 1718, Helena, MT 59624 or calling 1-800-582-2665. Also, please ask for a free copy of our current catalog listing all TwoDot® books. Visit our website at www.FalconOutdoors.com or contact us by e-mail at falcon@falcon.com.

© 1999 Falcon® Publishing, Inc., Helena, Montana
TwoDot is an imprint of Falcon® Publishing, Inc.
Printed in Canada.

1 2 3 4 5 6 7 8 9 0 TP 04 03 02 01 00 99

Cover and inside art by Lisa Harvey.

Library of Congress Cataloging-in-Publication Data

Pletcher, Larry, 1946-
  It happened in Massachusetts / Larry B. Pletcher.
     p.   cm.
   ISBN 1-56044-846-6 (pbk.)
   1. Massachusetts—History Anecdotes. I. Title.
  F64.6.P54   1999
  974.4—dc21   99-25063
                                                                   CIP

The publisher gratefully acknowledges David Allen Lambert, Librarian, New England Historic Genealogical Society, Mass. for reviewing this manuscript for historical accuracy.

Contents

CHAPTER ONE

The Survival of New Plymouth
· 1623 ·

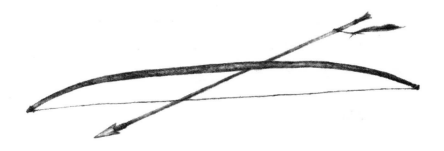

Dropped onto the shore of Plymouth Bay in December of 1620, only half the passengers on the Mayflower lived through the first winter. Greeted by sickness and harsh conditions, each Pilgrim needed to have the skills of a carpenter, farmer, pioneer, and soldier merely to survive. In 1621, with the help of a tribe of Wampanoag Indians, the Pilgrims managed to host the first Thanksgiving, but the true test of survival came the following year.

After being shot at while exploring Cape Cod and spied on while settling Plymouth, the Pilgrims already knew that not all the Indians were friendly. Allied by treaty with Massasoit, chief of the Wampanoag, the Pilgrims were caught in the middle between warring Indian tribes. When Canonicus, chief of the Narragansetts, sent a clutch of arrows wrapped in a rattlesnake skin, Governor

Bradford got the message. In the minds of the Narragansett, the Pilgrims had to go.

A hostile threat demanded a firm response. Dumping the arrows and packing the skin with gunpowder and shot, Bradford sent the bundle back. He wanted to let the Narragansett know that getting rid of the Pilgrims wouldn't be that easy. While Chief Canonicus considered his next move though, a diplomatic crisis chilled the friendly relations between the Pilgrims and Massasoit.

Abducted by an English sea captain and transported to Spain, Squanto was the only survivor of a Wampanoag village that was wiped out by the plague while he was in Europe. Eventually escaping from Spain to England, Squanto learned to speak English and returned to North America before the colonists arrived. After befriending the Pilgrims, Squanto became their interpreter and made the treaty between the Pilgrims and the Wampanoag possible. Regrettably, though, Squanto was also dishonest.

Once before, Squanto had tried to replace Massasoit as chief of the Wampanoag by telling the Wampanoag people that the Pilgrims had buried the plague beneath a storehouse in the English town. Anytime they wanted, Squanto claimed, the Pilgrims could dig up the illness and destroy the Wampanoag village. As the Pilgrims' only interpreter and very influential friend, Squanto said the Wampanoag would be foolish not to follow him.

When Squanto's scheme failed, he tried a second plan. This time, while Squanto was conveniently out of town, he had one of his relatives run into Plymouth and tell the Pilgrims that Massasoit had joined the Narragansett and was coming to attack the village. Refusing to panic, the Pilgrims sent another Indian to investigate the matter. The story was a lie. Massasoit was loyal.

When he discovered Squanto's treachery, Massasoit became enraged, confronted Governor Bradford, and demanded the traitor's head. Bradford knew that Squanto was a liar and deserved to be put to death, but Squanto remained an important link between the Pilgrims and the Native Americans, no matter how unsavory. He was the only Indian who spoke enough English to negotiate a treaty or discuss complex matters. Understanding the value of his interpreter, Bradford refused to hand Squanto over, and Massasoit left in a huff.

Bradford's tough decision nearly cost the Pilgrims their lives. From Cape Ann to Martha's Vineyard, their old enemy Chief Canonicus along with Massachusett, Nauset, Paomet, Sokones, and Agawam Indians plotted a war against the Pilgrims.

Massasoit knew of the Indians' plot to wipe out the Pilgrims, but, still miffed at Governor Bradford, the chief of the Wampanoag chose to remain silent—until he developed a bellyache. Miserably ill and thinking he might die, Massasoit received a timely visit from a man named Edward Winslow and a few other Pilgrims. Slipping the point of a knife between the sachem's teeth with what he called "a confection of many comfortable conserves," Winslow worked a miracle cure. The broth made with corn flour, strawberry leaves, and sassafras that he gave to Massasoit settled the chief's stomach. Grateful and much relieved, Massasoit showed his thanks by telling Winslow about the Indian plans for war. The Pilgrims handled the rest.

The uprising ended before it began when, in March of 1623, a small band of Pilgrims ambushed the ringleader of the plot. The swift action by the Pilgrims sent shock waves through the local tribes. The Indians were so terrified, Winslow wrote, ". . . they forsook their houses, running to and fro like men distracted, living in swamps and other desert places: and so brought manifold diseases amongst themselves, where of very many are dead."

After this brief skirmish, the Pilgrims and Indians were at peace for fourteen years. With the help of timely musket fire and a homemade stomachache cure, Plymouth had survived.

CHAPTER TWO

King Philip's War
·1675·

On a cold night in January 1675, John Sassamon disappeared. Educated at Harvard, Sassamon was called a "praying Indian," an Indian who was raised as a Christian and schooled in English ways. Though a friend and counselor to Metacom (also known as King Philip—chief of the Wampanoag), Sassamon had last been seen telling the Governor of Plymouth Colony that Philip was plotting war.

A month later, John Sassamon's body was found caught under the ice in Assawompset Pond in Middleborough. He had died from a broken neck. The English suspected that King Philip had silenced the man who had betrayed him, but they had no solid clues that pointed to Sassamon's killers. Then, a witness accused three Indians who were members of Philip's tribe. Within seven days, the trio was charged with murder, tried in a Plymouth court, and hanged by the Plymouth authorities. Just two weeks later, Philip responded by burning the village of Swansea, and King Philip's War began.

By one measure, the gruesome war that jolted southern New England proved worse than the Civil War. In proportion to the population at the time, King Philip's War is still the bloodiest conflict America has ever seen. Twenty-five towns were destroyed, and thousands died in fifteen months of brutal fighting. Springfield, Medfield, Lancaster, Marlborough, Middleborough,

Deerfield, Chelmsford, and Taunton were among the Massachusetts towns that went up in flames.

But statistics tell only part of the story of this nightmarish war that almost caused the English to abandon all of New England. Beyond the death and destruction that results from any fighting, King Philip's War became an orgy of blood where sadistic torture and lurid abuse were inflicted by both sides.

After inept English leaders allowed King Philip to escape from the swamps that circled his home on the Mount Hope Peninsula, the Wampanoag chief recruited other tribes and spread the war throughout the region now known as southern New England. In the months that followed, guerrilla tactics, random raids, and sniper fire caused gruesome loss of life on both sides.

A small stream near the western town of Deerfield became known as Bloody Brook when Wampanoag, Nipmuck, and Pocumtuck warriors ambushed sixty militiamen as they paused to cross the water. Indian losses were devastating in the Swamp Fight of December 19, 1675, and the Falls Fight of May 19, 1676, where English forces overran villages and put every Indian to death.

The events in Medfield on the night of February 20, 1676, explain why English farmers lived in constant terror. In spite of protection from one hundred soldiers who were quartered in the town, a band of Nipmuck Indians crept out of the woods and infiltrated the village. As dawn broke, sniper fire picked off settlers one by one as they stepped out of their homes. Pebbles thrown at windows led to deaths on bloody doorsteps for settlers who investigated. Fire was the ultimate weapon, as families were forced to choose between death in a burning house or a desperate run for cover.

Scalping wasn't the worst fate an unlucky victim could suffer. Some captives were skinned alive. Fingers and toes were hacked off for use on a warrior's necklace. For both sides, displaying dismembered body parts became a favorite method of taunting the enemy.

Unable to plant and harvest corn while the war continued to rage, the Indians faced hardships and the pain of constant hunger. When the Mohawk Indians of New York resumed their feud with rival tribes loyal to King Philip, the war was nearing its end. Forced to flee the Connecticut Valley by the pressure of a two-front war against the Mohawks and the English, a weakened King Philip returned to the Mount Hope peninsula where a band of soldiers led by Captain Benjamin Church shot and killed the Indian leader on August 12, 1676.

As Sassamon's death began the war, so the death of King Philip brought it to an end. Predictably, though, this brutal struggle ended with macabre cruelty. Soldiers drew and quartered King Philip's body and hung the parts from trees. His hand was preserved in a bucket of rum to become a trophy of war. Carried to Plymouth, the head of the chief was hoisted onto a pole where the skull remained as a stern warning above the town for a full thirty years!

CHAPTER THREE

The Salem Witch Trials
· 1692 ·

By the time Sir William Phips arrived in the Province of Massachusetts Bay in May 1692, Satan was hard at work. Phips, the new governor of the province, reported that Puritans in several towns were sorely being tormented by witchcraft and the Devil. Scores of unfortunate citizens had been, according to Phips, scalded with brimstone, stuck with pins, dragged out of their houses, or carried over the tops of trees.

The troubles began in February 1692, when Abigail Williams and Elizabeth Parris, the niece and teenage daughter of the minister of Salem Village, experienced fits that left them deaf and dumb. The girls soon lapsed into hoarse, croaking nonsense talk and periods of screaming convulsions that drowned out the sound of the reverend's holy prayer. Quietly, to avoid scandal, a doctor was consulted, but no physical ailment seemed to bother the two girls. The afflictions, the reverend and doctor concluded, were caused by the Devil himself and a throng of helpful witches.

The affliction spread rapidly to other girls in Salem Village before church members finally discovered that many of the afflicted children had secretly met with Tituba, the Parris family's West Indian slave. Curious about love and future husbands, the adolescent women had passed the long New England winter telling fortunes, learning tricks, and casting spells brought back from the Caribbean. Facing intense pressure to blame the Devil for causing the trouble rather than the girls, Tituba cleverly understood that fictional stories would satisfy her masters. To keep from being harassed, she shocked the church leaders with strange tales of red cats with human faces, a man with a book of names, and floating specters of village women that told her to harm the children. She confessed to being a witch.

Stories of Salem witchcraft sound fictional today, but belief in the Devil was once common in Europe and North America. Struggling against the hardships of a dangerous frontier and guided by severe doctrines of strict religious teachings, Puritans in Massachusetts believed the Devil lurked within everyone. Only vigilance and God's grace prevented any person from being bound by chains of darkness. To doubt the existence of the Devil was the same as doubting their culture, their religion, and their God.

Witch hysteria raged through Salem Village and infected nearby towns. Trials of witches were not really unusual at the time, but why an ordinary witch trial was blown out of proportion may never be fully explained. Financial stress, beleaguered farms, threats of attack from Indians, the need for love and attention of developing teenage girls, food poisoning, a community split by land claims, religious rivalry, and assorted petty disputes may all have played a part. For whatever reason, the adults needed scapegoats, and the children beset by witches were glad to give them a list.

Between February and June 1692, hundreds of innocent citizens were hauled before panels of judges, confronted by screaming girls, and thrown into prison to wait for formal trials. In the beginning, only those on the fringe of society were targets of accusations. Tituba, the black slave; Sarah Good, the sullen beggar; and Sarah Osborne, the loose woman who hadn't attended church, were the first women accused. But New England's inquisition swiftly climbed the social ladder; John

Proctor, a tavern owner, George Burroughs, a former minister, and several town selectmen soon were accused as well.

Governor Phips convened a special court to hear and decide the Salem cases, named Lieutenant Governor William Stoughton to be the man in charge, and promptly got out of town. Stoughton was a law-and-order judge who sternly conducted the trials without questioning "spectral" evidence. The Devil, he believed, could not assume the shape of an innocent person. When afflicted girls testified that they saw the shape (or specter) of the accused floating in the air, torturing babies, or tempting men by hovering over their beds, Stoughton was convinced. When a few other judges needed additional proof, the "touch test" was devised to confirm the spectral findings. If hysterical girls calmed at the touch of the defendant, the Devil had left the afflicted body of a girl and jumped back into the body of the accused. If the girl calmed when touched, the defendant was condemned.

Bridget Bishop, a flashy-dressing tavern keeper, was the first to be tried on June 2nd and hanged on June 10th. Hearing of the execution, Governor Phips questioned the court's reliance on spectral evidence and asked the advice of several prominent ministers in Massachusetts who urged the court to be careful and avoid being tricked by evidence from the Devil.

Seeing that trouble was brewing, Stoughton stepped up the pace of the prosecutions. In the single day of June 29, 1692, five more witches were tried and convicted. From July 19th to September 22nd, eighteen convicted witches and wizards were hanged on Gallows Hill. Fifty-five people confessed to being witches. One man who refused to plead either guilty or not guilty was slowly crushed to death when a sheriff tried to force him to talk by covering him with stones.

Phips had seen enough. To encourage guilty pleas, witches who confessed were jailed but not hanged, while respected people who proclaimed their innocence were rapidly sentenced to death. Prominent ministers, like Increase Mather, were also expressing loud criticism about reliance on spectral visions and the lack of solid proof. The Devil, after all, might assume the shape of virtuous people to incite a fear of witchcraft and divide the children of God. And how could girls afflicted by Satan still honor their sacred oath and testify to the truth? Besides, wrote Increase Mather in an essay distributed to other ministers, God is the ultimate judge. "He never intended that all persons guilty of capital crimes should be discovered and punished by men in this life."

Sanity finally reigned. In October 1692, Governor Phips limited reliance on spectral evidence, stopped the executions, and dissolved the special court. Dozens of accused witches were released on bail, and the Massachusetts legislature established a superior court to hear all pending cases. Of the fifty-two witches tried in January of 1693, only three were convicted and Governor Phips stayed the executions that Stoughton zealously sought. The terror was at an end.

Eventually, the afflicted girls repented and begged forgiveness from the town for being deluded by the Devil. Governor Phips signed a general pardon, and in 1711, the Massachusetts legislature paid financial claims to survivors of those executed during the terror. The last official recognition of the "shocking" and "hysterical fear" behind the Salem prosecutions occurred as recently as 1957, when the Massachusetts General Court finally proclaimed that no disgrace or cause for distress should be attached to the descendants of anyone punished by the "Witchcraft Court."

CHAPTER FOUR

The Deerfield Massacre
· 1704 ·

Before the French and Indian War and the American Revolution, no less than four European conflicts crossed the Atlantic Ocean and brought bloodshed to Massachusetts. King William's War, Queen Anne's War, Governor Dummer's War, and King George's War were struggles between France and England for control of North America that terrorized settlers in the Connecticut Valley for nearly eighty years.

During most of this endless warfare in the wilds of northern New England, people in the town of Deerfield were directly in the line of fire. The town sat alone in a shallow, exposed valley astride an ancient corridor traveled by Iroquois and Algonquin. Forty miles to the east or west, there was nothing but wilderness. A settlement to the north of Deerfield had long since been reduced to rubble by French and Indian raids, so the undefended settlements at Hatfield and Hadley a few miles to the south were the only English neighbors that the residents of Deerfield could count.

By 1690, several raids by enemy forces had brought random violence and death to settlers in the Connecticut Valley. The siege was never steady, but once a year or so a family was killed on the way to town, a farmer was shot while taking grist to a mill, or a ploughman was simply captured and dragged off to Montreal.

At the height of Queen Anne's War, frightened residents of Deerfield turned their village into an armed camp. As rumors of advancing French and Indians filtered through the valley, settlers built a crude fort or palisade in the center of town. Ten to twelve feet high, this wooden stockade formed a solid perimeter around the meetinghouse and fifteen private homes—a few of which were fortified with gun slots and heavy doors. Any families who lived in a house outside the defense perimeter spent their nights as guests of some other family who had a house inside the palisade.

No one will ever know why a sentry failed to be at his post in the frigid pre-dawn hours of that last morning of February 1704. Perhaps the village didn't believe that 142 Mohawks and Abenakis supported by two hundred French troops would walk all the way from Canada and attack in the middle of winter, but that's exactly what they did. Approaching from the frozen river in moccasins and on snowshoes, enemy scouts simply walked on top of the snow drifted against the palisade, jumped inside the fort, and opened the northern gate.

Trying to destroy an outpost that extended English influence into a region that France desired, painted invaders swarmed into Deerfield looting houses, slaughtering livestock, and killing anyone who vainly tried to resist. Deerfield residents were killed by musket fire or hatchets as they woke to the sounds of screaming and shattering windows and doors. One family died of asphyxiation as their home burned over their heads. A woman was shot through a ragged hole chopped in her front door. Men, women, and children endured terrifying visions as members of their family were murdered before their eyes.

In the center of the village, two fortified homes held out for several hours until the glow of the fires around them brought help from Hatfield and Hadley. When the smoke cleared, fifty-six English settlers were dead and more than one hundred had been taken hostage. Nearly half of the town's houses had been burned to the ground. After the massacre, only 133 Deerfield residents were left alive in the smoldering town.

The grim toll of the massacre fell with the most cruelty upon Reverend John Williams who had been a minister to the people of Deerfield since 1686. Bound and taken captive when his pistol misfired, Reverend Williams saw his six-year-old son, six-week-old baby, and one servant murdered in his home. His wife was captured by Indians and died on the cold retreat to Canada. Dragged away as hostages, Reverend Williams and his other children were allowed to survive as prisoners in the vicinity of Montreal.

The harshest blow to Reverend Williams was the fate of his daughter, Eunice. Captive English children often grew accustomed to foreign ways, and this was the case with Eunice Williams. Converted to French Catholicism and married to an Indian, she chose to live in Canada for more than eighty years.

Two and a half years after their capture, a prisoner exchange returned Reverend Williams and fifty-eight other Deerfield captives to their resilient town. Thanking his captors for kind treatment and praising the power of God, Reverend Williams went on to write a book called *The Redeemed Captive Returning to Zion* that described the Deerfield Massacre and his personal ordeal. He spent the rest of his life serving as the minister to a town that rose from a massacre with pluck and perseverance.

CHAPTER FIVE

The Boston Tea Party
·1773·

Tea was big business more than two hundred years ago. But the business had its problems. Shipped from the orient by the East India Company, all tea that legally came into England was hit with a heavy tax. Then, in 1767, the British Parliament added a special tax on tea that was bound for the American colonies. Small as it was, this three-pence-per-pound duty touched off the Boston Tea Party and kindled a revolution.

At first, rebellious Boston patriots found little support for a boycott of tea, but the East India Company still faced its share of trouble. Smugglers were undercutting prices and its storerooms were bursting with tea. To solve its financial crisis, the company suggested new laws that allowed surplus tea that was imported into England to be re-shipped to America free of the usual import tax imposed on British tea. The plan would make the price of tea that the company legally shipped nearly equal to the price of tea that others smuggled in illegally. It would benefit everyone.

Parliament agreed. The Tea Act of 1773 reduced taxes on English tea imported to America. But Lord North, the conservative leader of Parliament, cited "political reasons" and refused to remove the special three-pence duty that was levied only on colonial tea. Preserving British authority to tax the American colonies, the conservative leader wouldn't let Parliament give the colonists a break.

In Massachusetts, the reduction of taxes was seen as just a trick that cast the colonists as second class citizens and deprived them of their rights. The Tea Act greatly reduced the price of imported tea but forced colonials to pay the hated three-pence duty that England would still collect. The colonists believed it was nothing but a sneaky scheme to make people in America accept Parliament's right to tax.

Throughout the American colonies, people responded to the stubbornness of Lord North who kept the three-pence duty. With handbills and newspapers, angry patriots unleashed a wave of propaganda. In New York and Philadelphia, consignees (merchants who purchased British tea and sold it in America) backed out of their contracts with British shippers because of the mounting pressure.

But Boston was a special case. Backed by a British governor who thought he had enough troops to suppress any rebellion, consignees in Massachusetts refused to yield an inch. The patriots turned from propaganda to violence and threats. After participating in a mass meeting led by Samuel Adams, John Hancock, and other members of a patriotic group known as the Sons of Liberty, an angry mob ransacked a store owned by a consignee. Merchants began to receive death threats from angry rabble-rousers.

On November 28, 1773, the *Dartmouth* anchored in Boston Harbor. It was the first ship to arrive in Boston with British tea since the Tea Act had been passed. After another public meeting demanded that the *Dartmouth's* tea be shipped back to England, a detachment of armed militia was sent by Boston's patriots to guard the ship now docked at Griffin's Wharf.

A waiting game favored the British. Under customs regulations, cargo could be brought ashore by military force if taxes weren't paid in twenty days. Three ships were now in the harbor, and time was running short. On the twentieth day after the *Dartmouth's* arrival, thousands of patriots met in the Old South Meeting House and tried for one last time to find a peaceful solution. The captain of the *Dartmouth* wanted to return the tea to England, so they sent him to see the colony's governor. The *Dartmouth* could only sail past the British cannons that guarded Boston Harbor if the governor approved of its departure.

Near dusk, the patriots learned that approval had been denied. A showdown was now certain. Citizens who previously had only wanted the *Dartmouth* to leave in peace now became a rowdy mob as they followed patriots who were dressed as Indians and descended on Griffin's Wharf.

The Boston Tea Party was far more than just a symbolic act. Thirty to sixty men in three crews boarded all of the merchant ships. As the crowd watched for over three hours, the men hauled chests of tea out of the holds, broke open the chests with hatchets, and dumped everything into the harbor. When they were finished, ninety thousand pounds of cargo floated in the water. Three shipments were a total loss. Not a pence of tax was paid.

From the British point of view, anyone who participated in the tea party was a burglar and a treasonous criminal. The identity of participants remained a well-guarded secret as Lord North devised a plan to pay the colonists back.

The Boston Port Bill and Coercive Acts of 1774 cut Boston off from its neighbors in an attempt to bring the city to its knees. This series of vengeful laws removed judges, replaced elected officials, limited town meetings, required that officers charged with crimes be tried back in England, and authorized the British to seize buildings needed to quarter troops.

But the vengeful acts of Lord North martyred Boston overnight. If tyranny succeeded in Boston, it was just a matter of time before liberty was lost in New York, Philadelphia, and

Baltimore. Just nine months after the tea party, twelve out of thirteen colonies met in Philadelphia where the first Continental Congress agreed to stop trading with England and boldly declared the right of colonial self-defense.

The road to revolution had been paved with a three-pence tax.

CHAPTER SIX

The Midnight Ride of Paul Revere
· 1775 ·

Most Americans know the story of Paul Revere's midnight ride. How a lone rider galloped from Boston to Concord waking colonial farmers with shouts of "the British are coming." How a brave but untrained militia answered Revere's call. How citizen soldiers faced the Red Coats across a bridge in Concord, firing the "shot heard round the world," and starting a revolution. The problem, of course, is that most events didn't happen the way we learned. The truth is more intriguing.

Trouble had been brewing for many years in the colony of Massachusetts. After the Boston Tea Party, the British Parliament cracked down hard on the colonists with stern, repressive measures. To prevent violence, General Gage, the British Governor of Massachusetts, planned to seize all the gunpowder stockpiled in the region.

Stung by British repression, the colonists organized. Long active in politics and community affairs, a man named Paul Revere joined one of a growing number of secret clubs that were formed to resist the British, and he became acquainted with Samuel Adams, John Hancock, and other leaders of the revolution. When a Committee of Correspondence was created to coordinate Boston's effort with patriots in other colonies, Revere volunteered to become a hard-riding messenger for the cause.

Paul Revere first caught the attention of General Gage in December 1774. Tipped off that British troops were on their way to seize munitions from a fort in Portsmouth, New Hampshire, Revere rode north over frozen roads to warn his colonial neighbors. By the time Gage's troops arrived, a colonial militia had raided the fort, carried off the gunpowder, and lowered the British flag. General Gage was very unhappy.

The next spring, General Gage secretly planned to destroy all the munitions stored in Concord, Massachusetts. Under direct orders from London, he also plotted to arrest Samuel Adams and John Hancock whom the British regarded as instigators of treason. A special detachment of British troops was instructed to search the highways for people like Paul Revere who might try to warn the rebels of the coming British mission.

When word leaked out that British troops were preparing to leave Boston, the colonial resistance swung into operation. The Red Coats had two choices. They could march down a narrow neck of land that connected the City of Boston to the rest of Massachusetts, or they could shuttle troops by small boats across the Back Bay. Whichever direction the British chose, time was running short and the rebels had much to do. They needed to set up a signal to let people know which way the British were coming, arrange for boats to ferry messengers across the Charles River, warn Adams and Hancock so they wouldn't be arrested, spread word of the British march as rapidly as possible, and organize armed resistance.

The whole world knows what happened next. Signals were arranged: One lantern would be hung from the Old North Church if the British were coming by land. Two lanterns would be hung from the church steeple if the British were coming by sea. Two lanterns would be hung in the church steeple to signal the Red Coat advance. Paul Revere ferried across the water past a ship of the British fleet. He then embarked on a hazardous ride on a borrowed horse and was chased by British troops. The beginning of the story is quite familiar. The ending is less well-known.

Most colonists living in Massachusetts still thought of themselves as British. To townspeople sleeping west of Boston, news that "the British are coming" would have made little sense. As he galloped through every village, Paul Revere instead shouted words that colonials found truly chilling: "The Regulars are coming out." This message warned the townspeople that a regiment of well-trained British troops was marching on their town.

Revere had accomplished only part of his mission when he reached the Clarke parsonage, where Adams and Hancock were sleeping not far from Lexington Green. Hancock and Adams didn't believe that a large expedition of British troops would march out from Boston just to capture them. Guessing that the real British mission was to seize the gunpowder in Concord, they urged Revere to continue his ride to warn the neighboring town. The second part of the story that most people don't know is the strange event that ended Revere's ride before he reached Concord.

As Revere and others rode toward Concord to finish their midnight warnings, General Gage's well-planned strategy finally paid off. A patrol of British officers actually captured Paul Revere, threatened and abused him, and placed him under arrest. Fearing that this advance patrol really did intend to arrest Hancock and Adams back at Lexington Green, Revere managed to talk fast and gain the upper hand. Challenging the British officers while a pistol was at his head, Revere let the soldiers know just how much trouble they would find if the colonial militia spotted them near town.

Alarm bells and musket shots from the direction of Lexington Green convinced the British patrol that their insolent captive was right—the colonial militia was stirred up and the British needed help. They decided it would be easier to sprint back to Boston without a captive in tow. After the soldiers stole his horse and stranded him on the road, Revere walked back to Lexington and ended his hectic night by convincing Adams and Hancock to get out of the threatened town.

In the end, General Gage failed to consider what history also forgets. Revere didn't act alone. By the time the first shot was fired across Lexington Green on the morning of April 19, 1775, most of eastern Massachusetts had heard the chilling news that British troops were marching out of Boston. In less than eight hours, an organized network of rebels had spread the word to a tough colonial militia that had gained hard experience in the French and Indian War. Forty-seven colonial regiments responded to Revere's call. The British Red Coats marched as far as Concord where they fought a formation of colonial troops gathered at North Bridge and were forced to retreat under heavy fire all the way back to Boston. Paul Revere is still a hero for his harrowing midnight ride, but his story also reminds us that America's revolution was forged by thousands of volunteers united in a common cause.

CHAPTER SEVEN

The Secret War of Robert Shurtleff
· 1783 ·

Like many citizens of Massachusetts, Robert Shurtleff became a Continental soldier to fight for liberty. Mustered into the army as a member of the infantry, Shurtleff joined the Fourth Massachusetts Regiment and marched ten days from Worcester to fight the British. Of medium height and build, Shurtleff fought with uncommon valor. From West Point to Yorktown, through two years of war, Shurtleff's companions never suspected that Robert Shurtleff, the infantryman, was really Deborah Sampson, the only female soldier to fight in the American Revolution.

As a woman in her early twenties, Deborah Sampson dreamed of changing her life. Taken from her family at the age of eight because of their poverty, Deborah struggled to earn a living working on a farm. Denied a formal education, she longed to see the world and taste a bit of what life was like outside of Middleborough. But Deborah had a problem. In America at that time, a woman who valued her reputation could never travel alone.

Fearless and independent, Deborah devised a plan. Wrapping a bandage around her chest and donning a man's suit, she walked through town as a gentleman. When her appearance didn't arouse suspicion, she knew her scheme would work. On a warm spring night, she slipped into men's clothing, walked out the door, and the woman Deborah Sampson simply disappeared.

Assuming the name Robert Shurtleff, Deborah wandered west to Taunton, slept under the stars, then circled back to Middleborough to ensure that she wasn't being followed. Resuming her travels, she enrolled on a cruiser and was set to sail from New Bedford, but she changed her mind and roamed north until her money ran out. Inspired by a sense of patriotism (along with the need for cash), she enlisted in the army in Bellingham under the name Robert Shurtleff and traded her homespun clothing for a blue coat, cockade cap, waistcoat, and breeches.

Just two months after enlisting, Deborah Sampson found herself in the thick of a dangerous war. Assigned to a scouting party, she fought in a small detachment that gathered information behind enemy lines. Skirmishing in the fields and forests of the hazardous Hudson Valley, her patrol was attacked by cavalry and battled marauding infantry units in close-quarter combat. Facing vollies of carbine fire and charges by enemy horsemen, her raiding party stood its ground, inflicted heavy casualties, and learned the horrors of war.

In a fight near Tarrytown, Deborah and her compatriots spotted horses without riders. Swinging into the empty saddles, they rode into heavy fire, cornered the British at the edge of a swamp, and captured several prisoners. Completing a job well done, Deborah reached up to wipe the sweat from her brow and instead discovered a stream of blood gushing from her head. She couldn't stand up when she tried to dismount, and she noticed that her right boot was filled with her own blood.

Seriously wounded in the head and upper thigh, Deborah feared the army would discover her gender much more than she feared death. She was carried over a saddle horn six miles to a military hospital where she received treatment for the wound to her head. She lied to the surgeon and didn't mention the blood that oozed from the injury near her groin. After helping herself to bandages, salve, and a silver probe, she limped to a private room and secretly extracted the musket ball imbedded in her upper thigh.

Long before her injury was healed, Deborah Sampson was back in action. By the time the war ended, she had collected a gash from a broad sword and another wound from a musket shot, but it was a different enemy that would soon betray her secret and almost take her life.

Dispatched to Philadelphia, Deborah fell victim to an epidemic spreading death throughout the city. Delirious with fever, she was tossed in a filthy bunk and was soon taken for dead. Bound for the undertaker and too sick to talk, she called attention to her desperate plight by gurgling in her throat. Springing to her bunk, a physician, Dr. Binney, tore open her coat and made the shocking discovery that the soldier's heart was still beating—but beating in a female breast!

Shared only with Dr. Binney and a hospital matron who arranged for a private room, Deborah's secret remained safe. She soon regained her health and resumed her military life. As the war ended, though, Deborah returned to Philadelphia and faithfully carried a letter from Dr. Binney to her commander in Massachusetts. The letter told Deborah's commander that "Robert Shurtleff" was actually a woman. Dumbfounded by the news, her commander let Deborah slip into an elegant dress to prove she was a woman. He then escorted Deborah Sampson among friends in her old regiment. Her secret now revealed to the flabbergasted troops, Deborah Sampson was awarded an honorable discharge on October 25, 1783.

Not sure how she would be received after her disappearance, Deborah got back into uniform to return to her hometown. Assuming another masculine name, she lived the life of a man until she met her future husband the following spring. In 1784, she married Benjamin Gannett and happily raised three children while working their homestead farm in Sharon, Massachusetts.

In 1792, John Hancock and the Massachusetts House of Representatives made Deborah Sampson the first woman in

America to earn a military pension. Their resolution noted with approval that "Deborah exhibited an extraordinary instance of female heroism by discharging the duties of a faithful, gallant soldier, and at the same time preserving the virtue and chastity of her sex unsuspected and unblemished."

CHAPTER EIGHT

Shays' Rebellion
· 1786 ·

Once kindled, the flames of revolution are difficult to put out. Just three years after the thirteen colonies became the United States, citizen soldiers back on their farms in Massachusetts took up arms against the merchants of Boston in a violent clash of cultures known as Shays' Rebellion.

Daniel Shays was reluctant to be a rebel. Even as he led 1,500 men into the face of federal cannons, his goal was fair reform—not revolution. But crushing debts and a legislature that ignored the pleas of desperate farmers sent homespun veterans into battle fueled by the same love of freedom that fanned the revolution.

When the War of Independence ended, the British required immediate cash for all imported goods. To meet their obligations, Boston merchants demanded payment from shopkeepers who sold their goods in rural towns. The shopkeepers, in turn, demanded payment from farmers who bought their supplies on credit. Gold and silver were very scarce, paper money didn't exist, and the crops farmers normally used to pay their debts were still in the ground. When the farmers couldn't pay, a wave of lawsuits followed. Livestock was seized, land was lost, and proud, independent homesteaders were thrown into jail for debt.

Veterans of the Revolutionary War, the farmers were not about to take the loss of their freedom lightly. At least seventy-three towns in Massachusetts petitioned their legislature to ease the financial stress. Farmers pleaded for laws to authorize paper money, legalize payment through barter, abolish debtor courts, and relieve them of unfair taxes. When the legislature ignored their pleas and sided with the Boston merchants, the farmers decided the government needed regulation.

After cutting their second crop of hay in August 1786, more than a thousand "Regulators" marched on the courthouse in the market town of Northampton. Armed with flintlock muskets and assisted by surprise, the disciplined farmers asked the judges to cancel all sessions of court until the legislature had a chance to act on their demands. Facing bayonets, the judges chose to adjourn.

As long as the courts were closed, no property was being taken and no farmers went to jail. Court sessions were soon canceled in Worcester, Taunton, Great Barrington, and Concord. From September 26 through September 28, 1786, Daniel Shays, a Revolutionary War veteran from the small village of Pelham, commanded the rural rebels in a tense confrontation with local militia on the Springfield courthouse steps. No shots were fired in the standoff, and once again the outmanned judges decided to relent.

Boston merchants heard the news and exploded with indignant rage. Anarchy! Insanity! The lower class was destroying the government. Left unchecked, they might even let the British return and take control again. The merchants believed stern measures were required.

In October 1786, Sam Adams and other political figures who had fought British tyranny passed a brutal list of laws to repress their fellow citizens. The Riot Act authorized sheriffs to shoot rebels on sight. Another act allowed the state to jail suspicious persons without a hearing and without bail.

Wealthy coastal merchants also responded to Governor Bowdoin's call to hire a special army. Under the command of General Benjamin Lincoln, an expedition of nearly three thousand men marched through January snows, resolved to open the Worcester court that Shays and his upstart rebels had closed the month before.

Without a supply of weapons, Shays knew that his rag-tag force couldn't stop the tough artillery units commanded by General Lincoln. The only chance Shays had was to seize the 450 tons of military supplies stored by order of Congress at the federal arsenal in Springfield.

While Lincoln and his army were still busy keeping the courthouse open in Worcester, three companies led by Shays and other insurgents occupied bridges and ferry landings outside the town of Springfield, cut off the federal arsenal, and trapped the troops inside. Shays planned a joint attack, but a message was intercepted. On January 25, 1787, over 1,500 rebels marched against the stronghold without the support they expected. Neither side fired its muskets as the rebels slowly advanced. Maybe, the farmers thought, the troops inside wouldn't have the heart to shoot their country neighbors. Cannons fired over their heads, but the insurgents continued their advance. Then fourteen rounds of cannon fire ripped into their ranks. With four dead and twenty wounded, the siege of the Springfield arsenal came to a sudden halt.

Rebels burned stores and harried merchants in Great Barrington, Stockbridge, and other towns in western Massachusetts for the next several months, but a growing number of government troops who were hired to crush the rebellion had the guerrillas on the run. Neither side in this battle of neighbors wanted bloodshed. Lincoln's troops chased the rebels all the way to the borders of New York and Vermont where the soldiers from Massachusetts had no authority to follow and the rebels were finally safe.

By June 1787, Shays' Rebellion sputtered to an end. Within a year, a new governor pardoned most of the rebels, the legislature passed a law that put an end to jailing for debt, and a more robust economy eased the financial stress. Like many other rebels who had fled their native state, Daniel Shays chose to live his final years outside of Massachusetts in poverty but in peace.

CHAPTER NINE

The Saviours of Scituate

·1814·

Necessity is the mother of invention, and wars make unlikely heroes. Both cliches proved to be true on September 1, 1814, when two young girls, acting alone, repelled a ship full of British troops—without firing a shot.

The War of 1812 didn't spark much enthusiasm in the people of Massachusetts. They thought that the British had been taught their lesson during the American Revolution. A second war against England seemed wholly unnecessary. While war raged in New York and Ohio, British warships enforced a strict embargo that strangled New England merchants. Cut off from its lifeline of trade, Nantucket Island even declared neutrality to avoid starvation.

Like it or not, however, the towns of coastal Massachusetts were caught in a state of war. As the winds of the spring of 1814 warmed into the breezes of summer, ships from the British fleet patrolled Massachusetts Bay between Cape Cod and Cape Ann harassing coastal towns. Longboats (or barges) would leave their mother ships and row into peaceful harbors demanding food and plunder. Blackmail was standard procedure. Pay two thousand dollars, four thousand dollars, or whatever the traffic would bear, and the British man-of-war would leave your town alone.

In early June, the British ship, *Bulwark*, demanded beef and vegetables from the people of Scituate, a town with a small harbor on part of the Massachusetts coast known as the South Shore. When the citizens refused to pay extortion and provisions were denied, British marines rowed into town and retaliated. Ten fishing boats and coastal vessels were burned in Scituate Harbor, as the English reminded local residents of the nasty things that could happen to an undefended town.

A militia was quickly assembled for local self-defense, but the captain of the British ship calmly assured the village that the violence of the raid would never be repeated. The coast remained quiet. As summer began to turn into fall, citizen soldiers went back to their farms and Scituate dropped its guard. Simeon Bates, his wife, Rachel, and the nine Bates children tended the recently built lighthouse on Cedar Point. Scituate was at peace.

At high tide, just after noon on a quiet Thursday in September, the peace was rudely shattered. As Abigail and Rebecca Bates, teenage daughters of the lighthouse keeper, completed routine chores while their father was in town, they watched in terror as a British warship anchored close to shore. Unarmed and without help, the children counted seventy-four cannons on the ship. The girls were desperate and alone. They knew a raiding party of British marines would soon leave the dangerous ship and make their way to shore. What were they going to do?

The girls had watched the militia train and immediately thought of a plan. Ducking into the lighthouse, they grabbed their father's fife and drum then went back down to the beach where they hid behind the dunes. As the English longboats rowed towards shore, Abigail and Rebecca banged on the drum and blew on the fife furiously and loud. Suddenly a signal flag flew from the English ship. Looking bewildered, the British marines rested on their oars while they listened to the song of the regiment that they thought was on the shore. Another raid on Scituate wasn't worth a bloody skirmish with an angry local militia. A parting shot from a British cannon fell short of the dunes and splashed into the water as the longboats slowly turned around and headed back to their ship. Abigail, Rebecca, and their version of "Yankee Doodle" had saved their coastal town.

CHAPTER TEN

The Leviathan's Revenge
·1819·

When Ishmael, Queequeg, and Captain Ahab sailed from Nantucket Island to catch the great white whale, they were only made up characters in a Herman Melville novel. But Melville served on a Nantucket whaler, jumped ship in the South Pacific, and knew life at sea. He knew Nantucket's rich tradition, the legends of Nantucket ships that sailed to distant seas, and the hazards of the whaling trade. As he sat in his study in Pittsfield, Massachusetts, he gazed at a rounded summit in the snow-clad Berkshire hills and envisioned a great white whale. As he wrote *Moby Dick*, he recalled the fate of the good ship *Essex*, and remembered true tales of Nantucket whaling that were more frightening than any fiction.

Whaling was a risky business. To capture any whale, six men in a small boat in the middle of a hostile ocean would have to leave the safety of a mother ship and row a fragile craft within reach of the dangerous prey. Attached to the boat by a long rope that looped around a post at the stern and exited through the bow, a razor-sharp harpoon would be hurled at the whale. Wounded by the sudden attack, the whale's options were few. Some harpooned whales would "sound," or dive deep, while men in the boat above spliced on extra line. Other harpooned whales would simply "run" for their lives, towing the boat in a deadly dash known as a Nantucket sleigh ride. Salt spray would fly from a sizzling wake as the whaleboat bucked in the waves, and men crouched low and clutched the rail to keep the craft afloat. Any whale, at any time, was capable of turning "ugly." A blow from a fluke could capsize a boat or knock men into the sea. A random collision could "stove" a boat, breaking a hole in its wooden hull and sending it to the bottom of the ocean. On very rare occasions, a whale might even "breach," or rise out of the water, and crush the small whaleboat with the snap of its massive jaw.

Every experienced seaman knew what a whale could do. But as Captain Pollard of the *Essex* discovered, one exceptional whale could change the rules of the game.

On the fifth cruise of the whaler *Essex*, Captain George Pollard sailed his ship from its home port of Nantucket bound for new whaling grounds off Peru's Pacific coast. With half a cargo of oil in the hold after months of successful hunting, the whaleboats were lowered one more time when the lookout on the masthead shouted "There she blows!"

The pursuit was on in the small boats, and the First Mate, Owen Chase, let fly with his sharp harpoon. But on that fine November day the sperm whale acted "ugly." Recoiling in pain, the eighty-foot whale smashed a hole in the boat, and the boat began to take on water. Stuffing canvas into the hole, the crew returned to the *Essex* and started to make repairs. Only then did the First Mate notice that the sperm whale was still lurking on the surface a hundred yards off the bow.

"Odd," thought Chase. Then he watched in horror as the whale disappeared and lifted its bulk to the surface again dead ahead of the mother ship. His frantic shout to the helmsman did the *Essex* little good. Rising out of the deep blue sea, this lethal leviathan was about to wreak revenge.

When the whale rammed the front of the ship, the *Essex* stopped with a mammoth jolt that staggered the ship's crew. As the whale scraped its massive back under the sturdy keel, Chase raised a signal flag to call Captain Pollard and the men in the other two whaleboats back to the desperate ship.

Circling downwind, the whale thrashed on the surface again, raised its massive head, and rapidly gained momentum as it started its second charge. Oak planks that were made to withstand the power of Arctic ice broke like pieces of kindling from the force of the mighty blow. Before the Captain got back to his ship, the doomed whaler *Essex* rolled onto its side.

A thousand miles from land, the crew cut away rigging and tried to recover what gear they could before the ship went down. Compasses and quadrants were retrieved for navigation. Casks of water, hundreds of pounds of bread, dry powder and muskets were loaded before dark. The following day the crew sewed sails and got the whaleboats ready. Two days after the awful collision, three thirty-foot whaleboats drifted across the equator as the *Essex* broke apart and sank out of sight.

Lashed together and alone at sea, the whaleboats now held twenty men and provisions for sixty days. The men figured that they had enough time to sail east and reach the distant coast. But seafarers know that winds are fickle and the sea is always unkind. By mid-December tropical storms had battered the whaleboats, sea spray had spoiled the food, and they were hopelessly off course.

By the middle of January, one man had already died and a boat full of men was lost forever when it blew away in a storm. Captain Pollard and First Mate Chase piloted the last two boats that also drifted apart as their crews slowly starved. On February 8, 1821, a man on Chase's boat died and his friends made a decision. Cutting the flesh away from the bones, the survivors sliced and cooked the body. The flesh of the sailor kept them alive until a British ship rescued them ten days later.

Captain Pollard wasn't as lucky. Facing starvation, he and his crew also resorted to cannibalism when they picked the bones of Samuel Reed on January 28th. By the next day, though, the four men who remained alive were still rather hungry. No rescue ship was in sight. They agreed to draw lots. One to be executioner, the other to be his victim. On February 1, the Captain's nephew was murdered, and a sailor died of natural causes just ten days later. Dining on the flesh of a relative and a member of the crew, Captain Pollard and Charles Ramsdell managed to stay alive until their boat was found by another Nantucket whaler near the end of February.

Pollard, Chase, and three other sailors returned to Nantucket Island, but the Captain himself was haunted by the ordeal and sailed only one more time. His career and spirit were broken forever by a sperm whale's harsh revenge.

CHAPTER ELEVEN

The Experiment at Walden Pond
· 1845 ·

Folks who lived in the village of Concord didn't always have a high opinion of the youngest Thoreau boy. Reserved and standoffish, David Henry grew up with a mind of his own but never seemed to accomplish much even after his parents sacrificed to send him to Harvard College.

Known as an odd-duck, the young man asserted his independence by reversing his given names. After graduating from Harvard, he quickly failed as a teacher and then began to hang around with the famous writer and lecturer, Ralph Waldo Emerson. A sharp tongue and a prickly character added to Thoreau's reputation as an eccentric, chronic loafer. His reputation wasn't improved when he accidentally set fire to a large part of the local forest in 1844.

Hiking along a wooded path, fishing on a river, or watching a corner of a farmer's field on the outskirts of the village, Thoreau found his inspiration in nature. He knew what the people of Concord were saying about him, but he thought that they were the ones who needed to change their attitudes and climb out of their ruts.

At the age of twenty-eight, Henry David Thoreau began a grand experiment to show his overworked neighbors how simplicity and independence could create a fulfilling life. On fourteen acres of borrowed land on the shore of Walden Pond, he built a simple cabin where he spent the most famous year in the woods in the history of American culture.

Thoreau's reasons for living at Walden Pond are often misunderstood. He wasn't a hermit. He wasn't conducting an experiment in wilderness survival, and he wasn't trying to convince other people that life in a cabin was best for them. For Thoreau, the wonders of nature held the key to spiritual truth. This passage in his book explains it best: "I went to the woods because I wished to live deliberately, to front only the essential facts of life, and see if I could not learn what it had to teach, and not, when I came to die, discover, that I had not lived."

Scrounging about for used bricks and boards, Thoreau built his tiny retreat for less than twenty-nine dollars. He furnished his waterfront cabin sparsely with a bed, table, desk, and chairs for friends who might come to visit. Before the house was finished, though, he got busy in his garden. This man, who the town considered lazy, planted and hoed more than two acres of beans, turnips, and corn. In his first year, he supplied much of his own food and sold the rest for profit.

For twenty-six months Henry Thoreau lived in his handmade home beneath pitch pine and hickory—a "neighbor to the birds" and "monarch of all he surveyed." While he gloried in the cycles of nature in the wild Massachusetts woods, Thoreau wasn't isolated. He often strolled the railroad tracks that passed by Walden Pond and nodded to men on the trains as he walked the mile and a half to town to enjoy social visits and home-cooked meals. He even left for a long expedition to the north woods of Maine, mapped the depths of Walden Pond, wrote a travel book, and spent a night in the local jail when he refused to pay his taxes.

Mostly, though, Thoreau found time to follow the varied paths of his fertile mind. The record of his grand experiment is preserved in the book *Walden*, which he wrote over several years. Filled with Thoreau's off-beat humor and sidelong view of life, *Walden* finds significance in games of hide-and-seek with loons, a mouse that ate a pine, and a clear body of water that acted as a mirror to nature and a window to his soul. After nearly 150 years, *Walden* remains an inspiration to people who follow uncommon paths or march to a different drummer. "Be a Columbus," Thoreau advises in his book—not of worlds but of thoughts, and always advance with confidence in the direction of your dreams.

CHAPTER TWELVE

The Trial of Anthony Burns
· 1854 ·

Anthony Burns made one mistake. When he wrote to his brother in Virginia, Anthony passed along the news that he was working in a store in Boston. He went to the trouble of having the envelope postmarked in Canada but forgot that letters from runaway slaves were opened by their former masters. On May 24, 1854, U.S. marshals arrested Burns, charged him as a fugitive slave, and jailed him in downtown Boston.

Abolitionists had long been active in Massachusetts, but the passage of the Fugitive Slave Act by Congress in 1850 pushed those who opposed slavery to the limits of bitter frustration. It was one thing to tolerate slavery in the South. It was another matter entirely to pass a federal law that forced citizens of Massachusetts to help federal authorities capture runaway slaves. To abolitionist leaders, the Fugitive Slave Act was nothing but a "kidnapping bill" that denied men the inalienable right of freedom and turned their state courthouse into a "fortified slave pen." The law, they thought, made "good citizenship a sin, and bad citizenship a duty." Outraged and insulted, thousands of people in Massachusetts swore to resist slave-catchers by any means they could.

A Boston crowd had helped a slave escape once before, so U.S. marshals were on the alert when they arrested Anthony

Burns. Bullies, convicts, prize-fighters, and brothel keepers were hired as a makeshift posse to guard the escaped slave who was jailed in the downtown courthouse. To make matters worse, the "kidnapping bill" left little hope that a captured man could be saved by legal means. If Anthony Burns was to avoid return to the "withering hell of slavery," the abolitionists of Massachusetts would need an ingenious plan.

At the last minute, a scheme was hatched by Martin Stowell and Reverend Thomas Higginson, leaders of the anti-slavery Vigilance Committee who scheduled a rally at Faneuil Hall on the night after Burns' arrest. U.S. marshals would be ready for trouble at the end of the protest rally but not at the height of the meeting. Higginson would wait at the courthouse. John Swift, a zealous young man with a strong voice, would interrupt the meeting. At Swift's pre-arranged signal, other members of the Vigilance Committee would storm out of the hall, lead a crowd to the courthouse, and free Anthony Burns.

Late in his life, Reverend Higginson still considered this improvised plan "one of the best plots that ever failed." The crowd was large and enthusiastic, but Faneuil Hall had only one exit. Ardent abolitionists who tried to rush to the courthouse were defeated by architecture. There was just no way that a large mob could leave the Faneuil Hall meeting fast enough.

After supplying axes for the crowd to break into the courthouse, Higginson waited to see a few running figures approaching from Faneuil Hall. With the help of another protester, he grabbed the front of a heavy beam that he used as a battering ram. Blasting the door of the courthouse off its hinges, Higginson rushed to an inner stairway and was clubbed by startled marshals. Screams, cries, and confusion reigned, and then a shot rang out. Higginson and a few compatriots were pushed into the street. Instead of providing reinforcements, the crowd had fallen back, shocked by the sight of James Batchelder, a hireling of the U.S. marshals, dead on the courthouse steps. By the time protesters recovered their senses, the marshals had drawn their guns. The raid on the courthouse failed.

The trial of Anthony Burns lasted three days. Irate abolitionists streamed into Boston from all over Massachusetts. Money was pledged to purchase Burns in order to grant him freedom, but Charles Suttle, the slave-owner, refused to sell his "property" and stood by his legal rights.

As the hearings progressed, arrests for rioting and disturbing the peace were common on Court House Square. Bullets riddled the building, but rescue was out of the question. The courtroom itself bulged with guards heavily armed with revolvers. A corps of Marines from the Navy Yard and two artillery companies patrolled the courthouse corridors with guns and bayonets.

U.S. Commissioner Edward G. Loring announced his decision on Friday, June 2nd, and the verdict was no surprise. As thousands answered the call of handbills posted throughout the state and gathered to "lend the moral weight of their presence" to protest the forced return of the fugitive slave, the city of Boston bent to the yoke of military rule. Federal troops cleared the plaza and armed detachments blocked all streets that led to the downtown courthouse. Special officers formed a hollow square around the prisoner while several battalions of National Lancers, Light Dragoons, U.S. Marines, cavalry, and field pieces of the 4th Regiment Artillery completed a secure column. Shouts, hisses, and groans greeted the armed guard as it marched through Boston streets that were draped with the black cloths of mourning. As Anthony Burns was led to a steamer that waited at Long Wharf, pepper spray and a jar of vitriol were thrown on the cobblestones and a coffin labeled "Liberty" was lowered from an office window.

Anthony Burns was the last slave to be tried in Massachusetts, but as Thomas Higginson noted, the bloodshed in Boston was the first in a series of violent events that led to the Civil War. Less than a year after the trial, friends in Boston were able to purchase Anthony Burns from a slave trader. Free at last, he attended Oberlin College, moved to Canada, and served as a Baptist minister there until the day he died.

CHAPTER THIRTEEN

The Great Fire
· 1872 ·

In 1872, the narrow streets and alleys of Boston's business district teemed with old tenement houses and new stone-faced buildings topped by high wooden roofs. The danger of fire was always present. Most of Chicago had gone up in flames just one year before, and the people of Boston knew what could happen if a conflagration ever got loose in their dense city streets.

In the gaslight era, Boston's modern fire equipment included steam engines—horse-drawn carts with coal-fired boilers that pumped water through fire hoses. Unfortunately, in the fall of 1872, the department's horses were sick with distemper and couldn't pull the engines. If a fire broke out, fire fighters and volunteers had to pull the carts by hand.

Repeatedly pulling carts with drag-ropes exhausted the overworked men. To save his crews, the fire chief changed the department's policy so that fewer fire engines responded to the first alarms. This meant that, in the first crucial minutes of any fire, the response by the Boston Fire Department was cut by eighty percent. Within a month, events would prove the destructiveness of the chief's new policy.

A few minutes past seven o'clock on the night of Saturday, November 9th, an ominous glow at the corner of Kingston and Summer streets caught the eye of evening strollers. A fire had broken out in the basement of a five-story building where bustles and hoopskirts were made. As curious crowds marveled at flames that took only a matter of seconds to jump to an elevator shaft, shatter windows on the third floor, and then roar like a freight train as they swept up to the roof, each person assumed that someone else had pulled the fire alarm. As the blaze raced through the building, at least fifteen minutes went by before telegraph wires carried an alert to the fire station at 7:24.

Obeying the fire chief's new policy, only one engine went to battle the enormous blaze. As other units rushed to respond to second and third alarms, flames engulfed the building. Breaking glass showered onto the street, and a block of super-hot granite crashed to the sidewalk and cut a fire hose.

By 8:00, the city of Boston teetered on the brink of disaster. On the opposite side of Kingston Street, dormers on rows of tenement houses were already beginning to burn. On the north side of Summer Street, high wooden Mansard roofs were licked by tongues of flame.

The corner of Summer and Otis Streets was the last line of defense. With furious effort in searing heat, firemen stretched hoses through perilous streets and dragged their heavy lines to dangerous upper stories. Dull thuds resounded in buildings as violent fires blasted from room to room. Great cascades of smoke and flame billowed from roof to roof. Explosions rocked the neighborhood as gas mains erupted, torching nearby buildings and sending iron manhole covers rocketing through the streets.

Then, as the fire grew more intense, the water system failed. With so many hoses running, no one hose had enough pressure to pump water all the way up to the burning roofs. A number of hoses were shut down so a few remaining lines could have enough water power, but this left several fire crews stranded with no water.

The intense heat of the fire created its own wind. A firestorm sent sparks and embers flying all over town. By the time the five-story granite building at Kingston and Summer streets collapsed in a ball of flame, the battle had been lost. A conflagration was loose on the streets of Boston.

Knowing that their businesses were about to be destroyed, merchants immediately tried to salvage whatever they could. Warehouses and storefronts were stripped of merchandise that was then simply given away or piled onto Boston Common. On block after block, frantic men struggled to haul safes and other valuables out of the fire's path. In those days, bank deposits were not insured by the federal government, so bank customers rushed to withdraw money or to snatch priceless papers and jewelry from their safe deposit boxes.

By Sunday night, the fire had destroyed a fan-shaped wedge that began in Boston's financial district and marched to the city's docks. Sixty-five acres in the heart of the city were reduced to smoldering ash. The area was so thoroughly destroyed that, after the fire, searchers couldn't find the places were streets had previously been.

Victories were few. With the aid of a new pumper engine brought in from Portsmouth, New Hampshire, the Old South Meeting House was saved from the flames. As the inferno roared all around the building and fire flickered in the belfry, a stream of water from the new pumper was able to reach to the very top of the meetinghouse and extinguish the budding flames.

Wide avenues and large buildings eventually slowed the fire's progress. After the mail was removed to Faneuil Hall, the fire fighters were able to hold the fire at the Post Office during a Sunday morning battle. A row of steam engines stopped the blaze at the Merchants Exchange Building as fire fighters made sure that the flames weren't able to jump across State Street's ample width.

Because the fire burned on the opposite side of Boston Common's open spaces, residents in districts like Beacon Hill never really felt threatened. Many people even thought of the fire as a great excuse to party. From near and far, curious visitors flocked to Boston to enjoy a holiday. Along with smoke and flames, fire fighters from Boston and surrounding suburbs had to deal with a large contingent of inebriated observers.

Bostonians are known for their independence. The city regarded the random event as a chance to widen narrow streets and improve water mains. Within two years, all traces of the fire were gone, and the city was in better shape than it had been before the fire. Even though contributions poured in from all over the United States, Bostonians considered them unnecessary. Every penny was proudly returned—complete with current interest.

CHAPTER FOURTEEN

Inventing a Speech Machine

· 1875 ·

Alexander Bell had always had an unusual interest in the mechanics of speech. The son of a Scottish language instructor who was the model for Professor Henry Higgins in the musical *My Fair Lady*, Alexander Bell carried on his father's system of "Visible Speech," a written code that symbolized the position of mouth, tongue, and lips to produce a spoken language. After moving to Massachusetts in 1871, Alexander opened the School for Vocal Physiology at the age of twenty-four and used his father's methods to teach deaf students oral speech instead of sign language.

As a professor of elocution at Boston University, Alexander Bell commuted from Salem to Boston and filled his spare time with an odd range of experiments that piqued his interest in sound and speech. While studying the "phonoautograph," Bell used the bones of a human ear to create a device that etched the patterns of sound waves onto a plate of smoked glass. In another experiment, he tried to create a harmonic telegraph which would convey multiple messages along a single telegraph wire by using several pairs of tuning forks matched at different pitches.

In the course of his experiments, Bell quickly realized that his big imagination exceeded his physical skills. He needed an able mechanic to build the new machines that his active mind conceived. In 1874, when Bell hired a local firm to modify his harmonic telegraph, he met Thomas A. Watson, a gifted craftsman who worked in one of Boston's electrical machinery shops. Inspired by Bell's imagination, Watson soon became an eager assistant. With extraordinary skill, Watson began to transform Bell's ideas into real electrical machines.

For weeks, Watson and Bell tinkered with Bell's latest device trying to make it work. The transmitter and receiver of Bell's harmonic telegraph were each made of a thin metal reed attached to a small magnetic field. The transmitter and receiver were then connected by a wire. Listening carefully in separate rooms in a quiet workshop attic, they tried to tune the metal reeds to exactly the same pitch. According to Bell's theory, his transmitter would convert sound waves into vibrations that would then be turned into electrical pulses and carried over a wire. At the other end, the receiver would convert the pulses back into vibrations that would produce an audible sound. Bell believed it would work if the reeds were at exactly the same pitch.

Bell and Watson weren't having very much luck with the device until one of the reeds got stuck on that hot June afternoon in 1875. Watson plucked at the stubborn reed trying to loosen it. Suddenly, Watson heard his friend Bell shout with excitement from the other room. Bell had heard not just an electrical hum, but the actual tone of the plucked reed at the other end of the line. In a flash of understanding, Bell realized that he'd stumbled upon a device that would transmit the sounds of speech.

Afraid that their discovery would be stolen by competitors, Bell and Watson rented space in the attic of a Boston boarding house where they could sleep in one room and experiment in another. Bell and Watson continued to modify their new device, and on March 7, 1876, Bell was issued a patent on the electrical speech machine.

As Watson and Bell continued to improve their speech machine, Bell accidentally spilled a beaker of acid. Startled, he grabbed his handy transmitter and summoned his trusted friend. "Watson, come here, I want you," he said into the transmitter. Bell's hurried call for help was the first intelligible sentence ever carried by telephone.

The potential of Bell's speech machine was apparent from the very start. At the Centennial Exposition in Philadelphia in May of 1876, leaders of the world were stunned by the new contraption that altered the limits of time and space. No longer would information travel only at the speed of ship or horse. No longer would people in the country be detached from city life.

In the months after the Exposition, Bell continued to perfect his "telephone" and received additional patents. Bell and Watson carried on the first two-way telephone conversation on October 6, 1876, and they conducted the first long-distance, two-way conversation just four days later between Cambridge and Boston.

Bell eventually founded the Bell Telephone Company, defended his many patents against claims by other inventors, and continued to work with the deaf. But the same restless curiosity that pushed him to new discoveries also caused Bell to have little interest in developing the company that he had founded. It was Watson who expanded the telephone business, while Alexander Bell went on to invent the hydrofoil, hold the land speed record, co-found the National Geographic Society, and even invent a "photophone" to transmit sound on a beam of light. Individually or with others, Alexander Bell was awarded more than thirty United States patents during his remarkably productive life.

CHAPTER FIFTEEN

The Blizzard of '88
· 1888 ·

W hen the wind howls and the snow flies in the eastern United States, someone, somewhere is bound to say, "This storm can't compare to the Blizzard of '88!" The famous storm that battered New England in 1888 still lives in popular myth—a benchmark of brutal weather to judge the rest of history.

Other storms have left more snow, and winters have often been colder. But a combination of deep snow, bitter cold, and relentless gale-force winds made the Blizzard of '88 a unique weather event.

The tempest that struck Massachusetts from March 11 through March 14, 1888, began as two separate storms. The first was a system of low pressure that dragged a bitter cold front east from the Rocky Mountains. The second was a cyclone of moist air that spun out of Florida and quickly headed north. The result was a record-breaking low that stalled over Block Island and swirled past Cape Cod. What amounted to a winter hurricane with ninety-mile-per-hour winds hurled massive amounts of moisture at a wall of frigid air. The cities of western Massachusetts were directly in the storm's path.

Temperatures were pushing fifty degrees Fahrenheit on Saturday, March 10th. The East had enjoyed a mild winter, and New England was ready for spring. Forecasters, who customarily took Sundays off, didn't see any trouble coming. At worst, they thought they might be in for a raw, rainy day typical of the season.

While rain and sleet pelted Boston, the first flakes of blowing snow fell on Springfield, Massachusetts, late on Sunday, March 11th. By 11:15 that night, the unwelcome storm had arrived in the city of Worcester where ten inches of snow fell by morning. In rural Massachusetts, snow drifts reached first-story window sills and farmers needed lantern lights to do their mid-day chores. The snow continued to fall Monday night, and by Tuesday morning, snow-drifts stood thirty feet high and touched the roofs of houses.

Western Massachusetts took the brunt of the monstrous storm. Springfield, Worcester, North Adams, and Northampton were buried with thirty to fifty inches of powder, but extreme winds and constant drifting made the snowfall estimate nothing but a guess. Exposed fields and windblown streets might be free of accumulation while a few feet away huge drifts hid an entire highway or rose to a second story.

The sharp drop in temperatures paralyzed towns in the western end of the state, but the slow-moving cold front left the eastern third of Massachusetts hovering just above freezing. Boston was mired in slush, and other towns along the East Coast suffered devastation from rogue waves and high tides that smashed shorefront properties, wrecked two hundred ships, and snuffed out one hundred lives.

In 1888, gas lamps lit city streets, horse-drawn cars rumbled through towns on iron tracks, telegraph wires and steam locomotives connected urban centers, and the modern miracle of telephone service was only just beginning. Newly dependent on the transportation and communication of a dawning industrial age, people who lived in cities suffered most from the awful storm.

Horsecars in Springfield were abandoned on snow-clogged streets as passengers staggered through wind-whipped pellets of snow that stung their skin like carpet tacks and froze to their faces and clothes. Railroad engines bogged down, engulfed in mountains of white, stranding homebound passengers with little food and little heat. Photographs taken after the storm show crews of men standing on top of snowbanks higher than locomotives. In Holyoke, the weight of the snow collapsed factory roofs.

Telephone and telegraph lines snapped from the weight of the snow, and poles fell like dominoes from the force of the raging wind. Communications to and from Boston were nearly cut off at the height of the terrible storm. Telegraph messages to New York and the rest of the United States had to be routed through London on the transatlantic cable.

Throughout western Massachusetts, travelers who arrived in any town on Monday morning were stranded by the afternoon. Rising to the occasion, though, most people who were caught in the massive storm survived with a sense of humor. In Springfield, Cooley's Hotel overflowed with men who cheerfully posed for photographs in walrus mustaches and tall derby hats. The Massasoit House saw singing and dancing late into the night, and saloons served as a refuge and refreshment stand for every needy pedestrian who struggled down the street.

In Worcester, Union Station was jammed with marooned passengers who camped in the waiting room, played poker, and devoured every bit of food the restaurant had to offer. A baby was born on a railroad car that was stranded outside Springfield, while store owners in Pittsfield and Northampton dug tunnels through heaping snowbanks to open their downtown businesses.

Trains were stuck up to seven days, and many farms were isolated for as long as two weeks. On railroad lines, rescue engines had to ram into mountains of hard-packed snow to free stranded trains. Shoveling crews cleared streets with back-breaking labor, and ox teams strained to pull wooden rollers to pack down country roads. Eventually, though, Mother Nature cleaned up after the storm. By late Thursday, skies cleared, temperatures climbed, and the strength of the mid-March sun revived the promise of spring.

When the Blizzard of '88 was finally over, it had taken four hundred lives. In an age when workers were usually paid just seventeen cents an hour, property damage from the storm topped twenty million dollars. But aside from the terrible loss of life and destruction of property, the blizzard acted as a wake-up call. Before a giant storm could cripple the East again, horse-drawn urban transportation made way for modern subways, and forests of overhead poles and wires were buried underground.

CHAPTER SIXTEEN

The Birth of a Winter Game
· 1891 ·

J ames Naismith was nine years old when his parents died of typhoid fever. He was only fifteen when he dropped out of high school to support his brother and sister by working in the lumber camps of Ontario's Ottawa Valley. Self-disciplined, hard-working, and very fond of athletics, Jim resumed his education at the age of twenty, finished high school in two years, and secured a valuable scholarship to McGill University. Graduating from college near the top of his class, he enrolled at Presbyterian College and worked his way through seminary school as a no-nonsense instructor of physical education.

Combining his religious training with his love for athletics, Jim headed to Springfield, Massachusetts, in the fall of 1890 to use his unique talents at the School for Christian Workers, a booming institution that trained young men from around the world to be YMCA instructors. Assigned to the teaching faculty, Jim taught bible studies and boxing and continued to play the same Canadian-style rugby football that he had enjoyed as a child.

By the age of thirty, Jim had faced a lifetime of challenges and had earned solid success, but nothing had prepared him for the problem that his boss handed to him in 1891. Facing a rebellious class of forty strapping young men who were bored with gymnastics drills, Dr. Luther Gulick, the YMCA's superintendent of physical education, assigned the class to Jim. The new instructor had two weeks to invent a new indoor game that would satisfy a grumbling group of tough athletes who had little else to do during the long, cold winter.

A brief attempt to interest the men in children's games brought predictable results. Indoor tag, dodge ball, and leapfrog merely irritated his surly students. Efforts to adapt baseball, football, and English cricket to the cramped indoor confines of the Springfield YMCA brought only broken windows and laughter from the class.

Jim had to devise a team sport that was easy to learn and safe to play indoors. Perhaps, he thought, he could pattern a game after his beloved Canadian rugby football but with less running in the small gym and no tackling on the wooden floor.

Combining a rock-throwing game he remembered from his childhood with a variation of rugby football, Naismith devised a new indoor sport that involved two teams, a large ball, and a small open target. When the janitor offered to give him two peach baskets that he had found in a basement storeroom, Naismith took them and nailed them ten feet up on the balcony railings at both ends of the gym. The baskets had to be above ground level, he thought, in order to prevent players from guarding the baskets by sitting on them.

With a list of thirteen rules, Jim was ready to let his class give the new game a try. That first match in the basement of the

Springfield YMCA would have looked very odd compared to basketball games today. All forty men in the class played at the same time, which meant there were twenty men on each team. One rule said that the man with the ball couldn't move to another spot. Travelling with the ball or hitting the person who held the ball were considered equal fouls, but free throws didn't exist. Instead, fouls were penalized by awarding the other side a point, but this point was only given if one team committed three fouls in a row before the other team committed any. A ball that went out of bounds could be put back into play by the first person to touch it.

Naismith's rough new game pleased his rugged class who dressed in long pants and flew off the court, crashed through the crowd, and scrambled far out of bounds to chase a wayward ball. Wire fences were soon installed in many gyms to keep the ball on the court, an improvement that quickly earned basketball players the fitting nickname of "cagers."

Because the open tops of the first peach-basket goals often tilted downward towards the court, early rules made it clear that the ball had to stay in the basket for a goal to really count. In the first game, a stepladder was stationed nearby to remove the ball from the basket, a chore done only once, when a student named William Chase fired away from mid-court and scored the only basket. In the following months, chains were attached to tilting rims or small holes were cut in the bottom of the baskets so a person with a long pole could punch the ball out. Incredibly, it took fifteen years before nets with open bottoms solved the ball-removal problem.

Most of the other rules Jim had come up with changed as the new sport grew in popularity. When players began to stretch the rules by intentionally dropping the ball so they could move to a new position, the first "dribble" was allowed. But the early rules specified that dribbling had to be done with alternate hands, and it wasn't until 1905 that a player who had moved the ball by dribbling was allowed to shoot. Backboards didn't exist in the early days, and they weren't added to help the players. Wooden boards were first installed behind the baskets only as a way to keep rabid fans from interfering with the players' shots.

James Naismith didn't always approve of the changes that were made to basketball's rules. He thought the addition of a center line and a ten-second rule to bring the ball past mid-court made the game too fast and rough. But the changes clearly contributed to the sport's incredible growth. News of the new game spread rapidly in YMCA's from coast to coast. While James Naismith moved to Denver to attend medical school and then served the University of Kansas as its minister and athletic director, the game that he invented exploded in popularity throughout the world. In 1897, the Amateur Athletic Union (AAU) held its first national basketball championship. In 1936, basketball became an official Olympic sport.

Not far from the basement gym where the game was first played, the Basketball Hall of Fame in Springfield, Massachusetts, still honors the memory of James Naismith, inventor of an indoor winter game that now ranks as America's most popular team sport.

CHAPTER SEVENTEEN

Lizzie Borden
• 1892 •

Lizzie Borden took an axe,
and gave her mother forty whacks;
When she saw what she had done
She gave her father forty-one.

Two victims were brutally hacked to death in a blood-splattered murder scene. The weapon was missing. There was a history of family conflict and a frenzy of media hype. The scenario may sound familiar, but circumstantial evidence, false testimony, and a rapid verdict made headlines around the world long before the O.J. Simpson case. The trial of the nineteenth century revolved instead around the slaughter of Andrew and Abby Borden on a hot August morning in 1892.

The mayhem began in the guest bedroom on the second floor of the Borden home near the center of the town of Fall River. At about 9:30 A.M. on that sultry summer day, Abby Borden was struck nineteen times with a broad hatchet or axe. Nearly beheaded, her body fell beside the bed she had been making when she was attacked. Incredibly, in that compact house, the gruesome scene went undetected for nearly ninety minutes. When Andrew Borden returned home, he lay down in the parlor for a late morning nap. At 11 A.M., he died without waking as ten strokes from the same weapon that had killed Abby severed his eye and split his skull.

No witness saw the crime. Two rooms in a small house were grossly splattered with blood, yet there were no bloody footprints and no bloody clothes. No one heard a thing. Andrew Borden was a descendant of one of the families that had founded Fall River. Fired by the certain knowledge that an axe-wielding maniac had just killed one of the richest men in town, the city went into a furor.

Three people had been present in the Borden home on the morning of August 4th: John V. Morse (horse trader and brother of Mr. Borden's first wife), Bridget Sullivan (the family's Irish maid), and Lizzie Borden (age 32, the youngest Borden daughter). Over the next one hundred years various newspapers, books, and even plays would conclusively find each one of these suspects guilty beyond a doubt in what may be the longest-running, most baffling murder case in the history of the nation.

An infrequent visitor to Fall River with a questionable occupation, John Morse was the first suspect. But Mr. Morse had left the house early on that morning and had not returned until after the police were already on the scene. With no obvious motive, he was quickly ruled out as a suspect.

Bridget, the maid, was washing windows on that fateful August day. The last time she saw Mr. Borden alive was when she unlocked the front door to let him back into the house. After the murders, Bridget acted terrified to stay in the Borden home, so detectives quickly found her a job with the keeper of the jail. Curiously, Bridget was never considered as a serious suspect and testified as a witness for the prosecution during the trial.

Lizzie did some ironing on the morning of the murders and said she was in the loft of the barn searching for fishing sinkers at the time of her father's death. But Lizzie's story was jumbled, and she had to admit that she must have been upstairs close to the spot where her stepmother's corpse lay hidden behind a bed.

Fanned by the local papers, mass hysteria grew. Perhaps a wild-eyed stranger had done the evil deed, or maybe a desperate businessperson had killed the penny-pinching, cold-hearted, most powerful banker in town. But why would an intruder kill Mrs. Borden first? How could a stranger hide in the house for over an hour without being seen? How could any person covered in blood dispose of an axe, and flee like a ghost through the middle of a busy town? The police were stumped and pressure was mounting.

Detectives soon discovered that two people had a motive. Lizzie and her sister, Emma, never liked their stepmother, Abby. A dispute over their father's money had blown up in the past. Clearly, the sisters were jealous that Abby was able to share the family wealth.

When Emma claimed she was out of town on the morning of the murders, the spotlight turned on Lizzie who had an arrogant attitude the officers didn't like. Reports surfaced that Lizzie had tried to buy poison at a pharmacy in town, and three days after the murders, Lizzie made a big mistake. With police outside her window and people milling about, Lizzie burned a dress she owned in the firebox of the kitchen stove.

The police had no physical evidence, but Lizzie Borden had been at the murder scene, her actions were very suspicious, and her alibi about looking for sinkers seemed, well, pretty fishy. The attorney general scheduled an inquest the following week. Behind closed doors, Lizzie was grilled for two days in front of a judge and prosecutor without an attorney present. She was placed under arrest soon after she testified.

Prosecutors must have known they didn't have much of a case. The attorney general pled ill health two months before the trial and left the case in the hands of the local district attorney. The trial lasted thirteen days, but most of the state's evidence quickly fell apart. The dress that Lizzie burned wasn't the dress she had been wearing on the day of the murders. The hatchet the police tested for blood proved not be the murder weapon. A detective falsely testified about a "missing" axe handle that was really found by police, and witnesses clearly stated that Lizzie had no blood on her clothing immediately after the crime. The "inconsistent" statements that Lizzie made at the inquest never reached the ears of the jury. They were thrown out because she had been forced to testify without her lawyer present.

To the delight of the milling crowds, the jury returned a verdict of "not guilty" in only about an hour. A Sunday school teacher and hospital volunteer, Lizzie was popular in Fall River. The Woman's Christian Temperance Union, suffragettes, and feminists rallied to her cause. Free as she left the courthouse, there was no reason to think that the legend of Lizzie Borden would take a final twist.

In spite of the jury's verdict, the affair continued to haunt Lizzie. Newspapers would not let the story die. Hounded by a curious public and rich with her father's wealth, Lizzie became a recluse in a fancy house on a hill. In time, the mood in Fall River slowly turned. People who once were pleased by the not guilty verdict reacted to Lizzie's detachment by shunning the wealthy heiress, and the gossip began to get ugly. Much to the shock of local society, Lizzie was accused of shoplifting works of art from a Rhode Island store and carrying on an odd relationship with a well-known actress of the day. Eventually, public opinion turned against Lizzie. The woman who had been viewed as the wrongly accused suspect in the most sensational crime of the time is now known through legend as the "Lizzie of forty whacks," who got away with murder and flaunted the fruits of her crime.

CHAPTER EIGHTEEN

The Wreck of the *Wadena*
· 1902 ·

Y ears before modern ships steamed through the Cape Cod Canal, beach-goers in Wellfleet or Truro could look to the east and see hundreds of sails dotting the North Atlantic. Coastal schooners and cargo ships sailed between New York and Portland, Maine, skirting the hazardous Cape Cod coast where sandbanks and unmarked shoals shifted from place to place with changing tides and winter gales.

In a long history of disaster, more than 1,100 ships wrecked within sight of this innocent-looking coast. Caught on a shallow sand bar hundreds of yards from the shore, wooden ships were pounded to pieces in the growling, white surf. High winds and frigid seas froze sailors in the riggings and scattered the remains of cargoes and crews along deserted beaches.

Industrious citizens of Cape Cod soon learned to make a profit from the tragedies nature supplied. Everything from crates of apples to firewood to bolts of English cloth washed onto their sandy shores. A wealth of goods was free for the taking—if you were quick enough. Whatever the salvage laws, there wasn't much the owners of the goods could do after a pile of ship-wrecked cargo was stashed in a Cape Cod barn.

As time went by, beachcombers were not content to idly wait for goods to wash ashore. Professional wreckers stood watch over the coast trying to spot distress signals from ships that were caught in storms. Wreckers were experts in small boats and familiar with local waters. To earn their livelihoods, they braved angry seas and often commanded high prices to pilot ships through dangerous shoals or free vessels that went aground. If all else failed, wreckers would save captains and crews then help themselves to all they could take from the holds of sinking ships.

But wreckers were not heartless. Members of most local families earned their livings from the sea. From Provincetown to Monomoy Point, wreckers shared great concern for the fate of shipwrecked sailors who often struggled to a lonely shore only to die of wind and cold.

In 1785, the Massachusetts Humane Society was created by Bostonians not to save barnyard pets but to save the lives of desperate sailors. The society built "charity houses" which were crude huts along the coast where seamen could stay alive if they washed ashore on a stormy night. Lifeboats were soon added to the list of standard equipment that were kept at the charity houses, and one hundred years later the role of these valuable stations was finally taken over by the U.S. Life-Saving Service.

By the early 1900s, thirteen stations on the Cape Cod coast were manned by government surfmen who were trained to row wooden dories through turbulent, stormy seas. Dedicated lifesavers who would come to the aid of captain and crew and not pilfer cargo, these heroes of the U.S. Life-Saving Service were competitors to the Cape Cod wreckers. Yet in spite of a lively competition to reach disasters first, wreckers and surfmen respected one another and the hazards of their similar trades. However, on March 17, 1902, when wreckers and surfmen crossed paths under dangerous circumstances, the courage of both would not be enough to prevent a tragic result.

A northeast gale churned the sea south of Cape Cod's elbow where the coal barge *Wadena* was grounded on a hidden shoal.

At the crack of dawn, Captain Eldredge of the Monomoy Life-Saving Station spotted a distress flag flying from the vessel's rigging. Springing into action, Captain Eldredge and seven surfmen immediately launched a surfboat, pulling hard on the wooden oars as they rowed against the crashing breakers and the sting of the icy spray.

Five men feared for their lives aboard the hapless barge as the sea roiled all around them and the sky spit flakes of snow. In their haste to escape to the surfboat, one man fell and broke a thwart that supported the crew when the surfboat was rowed. Ordered to lie on the bottom to keep the surfboat stable in the ocean's treacherous chop, the men from the barge lost their nerve when a wave splashed over the side. Standing in panic, they clutched at the helmsmen, capsized the rescue boat, and were flung into the freezing sea.

Twice, heroic surfmen accomplished the nearly impossible task of righting the overturned craft. But crashing waves kept rolling the boat upside down again before they could climb inside.

Elmer Mayo, a wrecker who sailed out of Chatham, was working another stranded ship when he spotted the keel of the surfboat awash in the churning sea. Reacting quickly, he jumped in a twelve-foot dory, grabbed a pair of oversized oars, and pulled alone through the blustery storm to save the struggling surfmen and the sailors they had tried to rescue.

But the sea was unforgiving. When Mayo arrived, Captain Eldredge, every member of the barge crew, and six of the brave surfmen had lost their grip on the capsized boat. Only one surviving surfman still clung to the surfboat's keel. The rest had lost their battle with the angry sea. The wreck of the *Wadena* resulted in one of the worst disasters in the long, proud history of the U.S. Life-Saving Service.

Six weeks after being rescued, Seth Ellis, senior surfman, became the new keeper of the Monomoy Life-Saving Station. Mayo and Ellis both received Congressional medals to reward their heroic efforts. Mayo returned to his dangerous work—now as the most famous wrecker to sail the Cape Cod coast.

CHAPTER NINETEEN

The Battle of Orleans
· 1918 ·

A hazy sun promised a steamy summer Sunday on the beaches of Cape Cod. High on a bluff above the shore, the owners of ocean-front cottages sipped late-morning coffee and gazed out to sea where the ocean tug *Perth Amboy* lazily towed four barges south toward Vineyard Sound. Suddenly, near the entrance to Nauset Harbor, an apparition appeared. With guns blazing, a German U-boat emerged from the foggy mist and fired the only enemy shells to strike American soil during all of World War I.

Attacking without warning at 10:30 on the morning of July 21st, the first shots in what newspapers dubbed the "Battle of Orleans" blasted away the pilot house of the slow, defenseless tug. As the deafening roar of shelling fractured a tranquil calm, twenty-eight men, four women, and two boys faced a bombardment of hostile fire at point-blank range. Luckily for the families and crews that worked on the stricken ships, the Germans were rotten shots. As shells continued to rain down on the small civilian fleet, twelve-year-old Jack Ainsleigh, son of a barge captain, stood defiantly on the deck of his father's boat and waved an American flag at the enemy U-boat commander. Hundreds of rounds of ammunition whistled through the sky, ripped into the wooden hulls of the boats, and threw up geysers of salt water when the gunners missed their mark.

Lured by the man-made thunder, more than a thousand spectators gathered on Nauset Heights to watch the shooting spree. As the onslaught continued, families and crews on the tug and barges piled into smaller craft, trying to escape the gunbarrel flashes that tracked them toward the beach. Wild shots flew over their heads and tore craters in the sand while the owners of seaside cottages helped the victims to shore.

Alerted by the din of exploding shells and the rattle of machine gun fire, crews from the Nauset Life-Saving Station and local lobstermen quickly launched their boats to help with the daring rescue. Though the shooting continued for an hour and a half, only two men were wounded when they were hit by splinters off bursting shells. It took the German submarine nearly two hours of constant shelling to set fire to the *Perth Amboy*, sink two empty barges, and send a load of New England granite to the bottom of the sea.

The American response to the dastardly attack was equally ineffective. Streaking into the fray from the Chatham Naval Air Station, three military airplanes circled over the U-boat, dodged anti-aircraft fire (that missed its mark), and dropped three payloads of bombs—all of which were duds. Ending the noisy battle, the German submarine then re-submerged and continued it journey south.

While smoke rose from the burning tug and a barge drifted stern up with its bow under water, people on shore realized that a member of the crew was missing. Suspecting that his long-time friend was still on the barge, Captain Ainsleigh planned to sail out to the smoking wreck the next morning. However, the Captain was spared the trip. Yelping a call for help, Rex, the missing barge dog, caught the attention of a fishing boat and hitched a ride to shore.

CHAPTER TWENTY

The Great Molasses Flood

• 1919 •

The mid-winter sun shone bright and clear on Boston's North End. Workers at the busy railroad sheds looked forward to a noontime break, and horses in the Public Works stable were content with their grain and hay. After a frigid low of two degrees Fahrenheit just a few days before, the temperature was in the forties. Cats snoozed in the brilliant sun, and workmen turned to face the sky as they ate their lunch outside.

Tenement buildings, small shops, and freight sheds stood side by side in the active neighborhood where Commercial Street curled past the docks on the Charles River. It was in this neighborhood that the storage tank of the Purity Distilling Company stood two blocks north of the Old North Church and across the river from the Charlestown Navy Yard where *Old Ironsides* rests today. On the day of the great flood, a passenger train had just clattered through this neighborhood on its elevated track, when a dull, muffled rumbling sound shook the earth. Cast iron was tearing and rows of rivets were popping like machine-gun fire. The distilling company's fifty-eight-by-ninety-foot storage tank filled with yellow-brown molasses was bursting at its seams.

Whoever coined the expression "slow as molasses in January" didn't count on a two-million-gallon tank exploding under the pressure of four thousand pounds per square foot. Flying sheets of cast iron ripped into the elevated railroad tracks and crumpled a section of trestle. Released from its confinement, gushers of soaring molasses blasted into the streets with unbelievable speed. For anyone in the neighborhood, there was simply no escape.

The force of the blast demolished several tenements, crushed a typewriter store, and hurled a loaded boxcar through the wall of a railroad shed. A rogue, eight-foot-high wave of molasses slammed into the side of a terminal building and shoved four heavy freight cars down the track. Like a bulldozer gone berserk, the unstoppable weight of this torrent of goo knocked a firehouse and several warehouses completely off their foundations and pushed them toward the harbor.

Some people were killed instantly, flung about like rag dolls, dashed against freight cars, or crushed by falling debris. Others died a slower death in the grasp of the clutching sludge. Men, women, children, and horses running in the streets were overtaken by sticky ooze, stopped in their tracks, and sucked to a sticky fate.

Five men in the Public Works Building drowned in molasses as they ate their lunch, but the most gruesome loss of life took place in a railroad shed. Trapped in a cramped basement when a five-foot flood of molasses swept across the floor above, several railroad workers heard walls crash and men scream above their heads. A tidal wave of molasses tossed any freight that was in its path, submerged the whole first floor of the railroad shed, and then began to flow down the only stairway to the basement. The men in the basement could hear the wooden beams above their heads groaning and creaking under the immense weight of the molasses. Then, suddenly, barrels, boxes, and tons of molasses crashed through the floor above and buried them without a trace.

In just a few minutes of mayhem, the Great Molasses Flood killed twenty-one people and injured 150. A dozen horses died while they ate their hay in the stable or pulled carts through the busy neighborhood streets. The city began to clean up with fire hoses right away, but gooey reminders fouled Boston Harbor and clung to the cobblestone streets for well over six months.

Officials never found out why the tank of molasses exploded that day. Perhaps the tank had been overfilled, or perhaps the molasses had created excess pressure by expanding in the warmer weather. Whatever the explanation, in typical American fashion, the episode ended up in court. After years of litigation, blame was fixed on the United States Industrial Alcohol Company, the parent company that owned the tank. In the end, the distilling company paid out almost one million dollars to settle 125 claims for all the death and destruction caused by the Great Molasses Flood.

CHAPTER TWENTY-ONE

The Boston Police Strike
·1919·

Pay scales for Boston patrolmen were twenty years out of date. Outfitted in domed caps and wing-collared coats that made them look like Keystone Cops, Boston police were forced to work seventy-three hours a week for only twenty-nine cents an hour. They only got one day off every nine days, and they had to sleep two to a bed in vermin-infested stations. Deciding to take action, the Boston Social Club, the local police organization, joined hands with a national union, the American Federation of Labor (AFL).

While labor unrest plagued the nation at the end of World War I, Boston was in the middle of a political transformation. Upstart Irish Democrats had wrested city hall from the grasp of the wealthy Republicans who ran the rest of the state. But upper-crust patricians still controlled the police department through the office of a commissioner who answered to the governor rather than the mayor.

Determined to show firm command and teach the Irish a lesson, Police Commissioner Edwin Curtis forbade the Boston Social Club from associating with the AFL or any other union. Police, he said, weren't employees but duty-bound officials. They owed allegiance to the public, not to a labor union, Police Commissioner Curtis said, and when he suspended nineteen men for leading the union movement, all but two union members voted to strike the following day.

As three quarters of the police force turned in their badges and walked out the door, politicians passed the buck and tried to shift the blame. Confident as ever, Curtis, thinking he was still in control, lined up volunteers to assist the few police who remained on active duty. Deprived of power, the mayor of Boston begged Governor Calvin Coolidge to call out the State Guard. Lethargic to the core, "silent Cal" responded by sending troops home. The governor made it quite clear that the problem really wasn't his.

With most of the police officers on strike, high jinx and youthful pranks took over the streets of Boston. Restless crowds of teenage rowdies roamed the thoroughfares and pelted police stations with mud, eggs, and ripe fruit stolen from pushcart vendors. Flaunting their freedom from the law, hooligans sounded false alarms and gambled in the numerous crap games that sprang up on Boston Common. They threw rocks and bricks through plate glass windows, and looted and plundered the undefended streets. Slowly, the city crossed the invisible line that separates order from chaos.

In order to deal with the crime wave, the city of Boston turned into an armed camp. Students from Harvard College were issued badges and guns, but the college kids were no match for all of the criminals that headed for Boston's streets. At Scollay Square, five thousand rioters cornered a few of the police volunteers, relieved them of their weapons, and were about to beat them up when long-delayed reinforcements finally reached the scene. Just in time, the First Troop of Cavalry of the Massachusetts State Guard thundered into the square, parted the crowd with sabers drawn, and rescued the young recruits.

Barbed wire and armed guards protected banks and stores, while 4,700 guardsmen patrolled the troubled Boston streets. On Broadway in South Boston, riot troops fired warning shots over a swirling mob. Retorts of scattered pistol fire echoed in return. Taunting jeers, then rocks and bottles flew at the troops, and the captain in charge was felled by a rock that struck him in the head. The guardsmen fired on the mob.

After two days of mayhem, eight civilians were dead, twenty-one were wounded, and fifty others injured. The guard had gained control of the city, and the striking policemen quickly voted to bring the strike to an end.

Because of the mobs that had plagued the streets, most people in Massachusetts agreed with President Woodrow Wilson when he said the police walkout wasn't a strike, it was a crime against civilization. When policemen asked to return to work, each one who had gone on strike was fired. Their jobs were filled by replacements who received the additional pay of only three hundred dollars per year. Fifty years would pass before any police department in the country would try to strike again.

In a telegram to the AFL after the strike, the governor of Massachusetts proudly crowed, "There is no right to strike against the public safety by anybody, anywhere, any time." The man of few words had stumbled upon the perfect media quote. The sentiment captured the public's mood and catapulted Calvin Coolidge to the presidency of the United States.

CHAPTER TWENTY-TWO

The Curse of the Bambino
·1920·

It was the bottom of the tenth in game six of the 1986 World Series. There were two outs, nobody on, and two strikes on the hometown batter. The visitors from Boston had forged ahead five to three in the top of the extra inning. Leading the series three games to two, the Red Sox were only one strike away from their first World Series championship in sixty-eight years.

Then, a couple of solid singles whispered the voice of doom, and veteran watchers of Boston baseball knew what lay ahead. The Boston pitcher looked scared. Another hit to center field brought the Mets within one run. Then, a new Boston hurler tied the game when he fired a wild pitch and a runner scored from third. The end was surely near, but a ball tapped down the first base line gave Boston a ray of hope.

Fans may never forgive Red Sox first baseman Bill Buckner for letting that grounder dribble between his legs, but fans must always remember that a powerful force helped the New York Mets defeat their team that day. Reaching all the way from Fenway Park in Boston to Shea Stadium in New York, the Curse of the Bambino had jinxed the Red Sox again.

There was a time when Boston was the powerhouse of baseball. Long before the Bronx Bombers turned New York into baseball's capital city, Boston was the team to beat. Long before Gehrig, Dimaggio, Maris, and Mantle made the Yankees America's team, New England was the home of champions. The Boston Pilgrims was one of the teams that founded the American League. All-time great Cy Young was a Hall-of-Fame Boston pitcher. Renamed the Red Sox and playing in Fenway Park, the team from Boston won five out of seven World Series championships in the years between 1912 and 1918. But in 1920, the owner of the Red Sox made a terrible mistake.

George Herman "Babe" Ruth was more than a promising pitcher. The big lefty had already piled up 29.2 consecutive shutout World Series innings while playing for the Boston team. The "Bambino" was also a good hitter and the heart of the Boston team. But Harry Frazee, who owned the team, needed one hundred thousand dollars to finance a Broadway play. When the wheeling and dealing was over, Babe Ruth, in effect, was traded to the New York Yankees in exchange for the Broadway musical *No, No, Nanette*. On January 3, 1920, the Curse of the Bambino was born.

Babe Ruth would propel the Yankees to the top of the baseball heap. After a few years, you'd think that the sale of a star player would be overcome, but the sale of the Sultan of Swat, the greatest home-run hitter in the history of the American League, cast a spell over Fenway Park. The betrayal by that early owner still lingers to the present day. Because of the curse, baseball in Fenway Park has never been the same.

The strength of the curse can be judged by the greatness of the players who have failed to break its spell. Ted Williams, the last .400 hitter in major league baseball, Roger Clemens, the single-game strikeout king, and superstars like Carl Yastrzemski, Carleton Fisk, Wade Boggs, and Jim Rice never broke the jinx. The vaunted Red Sox lost the World Series in seven games to the St. Louis Cards in 1946, again in 1967, and suffered the same agony when they lost game seven of the World Series to Cincinnati in 1975. In a one-game playoff in 1978, a light-hitting Yankee shortstop kept the Red Sox out of the series with a heart-breaking pop-up homer into Fenway's left field screen. Since the start of the curse, the rival New York Yankees have won thirty-one World Series titles. Since the start of the curse, the Red Sox have won none.

Rain delayed the last game of the 1986 World Series, but game seven was really just an afterthought. Taunting Boston with a victory that seemed so near yet far away, game six had proven beyond a doubt that the curse was still alive. Playing under the weight of an evil spell, the Red Sox season ended again with a loss of eight to five.

The power of the curse continues to the present day. Some say the town of Mudville in the poem "Casey at the Bat" characterizes Boston, a city that still cheers after eighty years trying to break a curse.

CHAPTER TWENTY-THREE

The Death of the Swift River Valley

· 1927 ·

Imagine a disaster that completely destroyed four towns, displaced thousands of people, and drowned an entire valley. Homes, factories, and schools leveled, highways and railroads cut. Tops of rolling mountains reduced to mere islands scattered in an inland sea. Now imagine that this devastation of thirty-six square miles was intentionally caused by man.

The story of the Quabbin Reservoir is the story of just such a disaster.

Isolated on a spit of land on the edge of a saltwater harbor, people living in Boston were thirsty from the very start. Efforts to find a reliable source of fresh water began as early as 1652, when settlers constructed a wooden reservoir in what is now the center of town. Frequent fires and a growing population reinforced the need for potable water, and the city first reached beyond its boundaries to tap into a neighboring pond in 1795.

The Civil War brought expanded trade to the busy port of Boston, and industrial growth late in the 1800s swelled the surrounding suburbs. City politicians soon understood that two hundred years of hard work had really done little to slake metropolitan Boston's thirst.

Enfield, Greenwich, Dana, and Prescott were sleepy rural towns in the last half of the nineteenth century. The people in those towns ran family farms or small country businesses that sound quaint to our ears today. Gristmills, box factories, harness shops, a hat company, and a maker of pewter buttons were part of the rural scene. Scattered throughout the Swift River Valley seventy-five miles west of Boston, residents of these small mid-state towns found it easy to ignore the ominous signs that their way of life might need to suffer for the sake of Boston's good.

When the legislature focused its attention on the Swift River as a possible source for the water that Boston needed, a political battle ensued. Representatives of the Swift River Valley ranted about the threat to the valley's small towns. Urban politicians bellowed their demands for alternate sources of water to fuel the city's growth. A few faint voices even called for conservation, and a legal challenge went all the way to the U.S. Supreme Court.

In the struggle for power, Boston had all the muscle. Even the residents of the valley could predict the end result. On April 26, 1927, the legislature passed the Swift River Act, authorized the Quabbin Dam, and doomed the Swift River Valley. With sorrow, mourning, lamentations, but remarkably little anger, the citizens of Enfield, Greenwich, Dana, and Prescott prepared to watch their towns die.

The preliminary work of surveying land, photographing buildings, confirming ownership of property, and planning ways to relocate roads lasted several years. Some residents of the valley towns left as soon as they could, but many didn't relocate until 1936, at the height of the Great Depression. Displaced owners were paid for their property that was taken, of course, but most folks took only what the government offered and didn't object.

The Swift River Act called for construction of a giant dam to block the Swift River. As construction began on Quabbin Dam, immense blocks of reinforced concrete sixteen feet high, nine feet wide and forty-five feet long were sunk to bedrock ledge. Men worked in chambers beneath these massive caissons, digging out earth and gravel until each block sank 135 feet down to solid rock. Once this watertight row of concrete blocks stretched 2,640 feet across the length of the dam, four million cubic yards of clay, sand, and gravel were spread on top to finish the enormous job.

As the dam neared completion, the hurricane of 1938 tested its construction. The dam withstood the storm. In July 1939, the river was finally impounded, and 412 billion gallons of water gathered behind the dam. The Swift River Valley was flooded, and the unquenchable thirst of Boston had at last been satisfied.

Today, the Quabbin Reservoir is surrounded by a reservation of 85,000 acres. Home to bald eagles, rainbow trout, coyotes, and many deer, it preserves a place of resurgent nature and haunting memories.

CHAPTER TWENTY-FOUR

The Execution of Sacco and Vanzetti
· 1927 ·

Men who worked in the shoe factories of South Braintree, Massachusetts, were always paid in cash. As Frederick Parmenter, the paymaster, and Alessandro Berardelli, his guard, walked with boxes of payroll money from the offices of Slater & Morrill to the company's factory building, two bandits circled behind them and shot them both in the back. In the broad daylight of mid-afternoon on April 15, 1920, Berardelli fell to his knees by the side of the road where one of the gunmen finished him off. Hit once, Parmenter dropped the cash and staggered across the street where a second shot ended his life.

The crime took less than five minutes. A third bandit fired a shotgun blast to keep bystanders at bay. Then a touring car holding two more outlaws motored up the street. Bullets sprayed from the getaway car as the gunmen scooped up the cash and sped away from the scene.

Two days later, police found a stolen Buick in the woods of a nearby town. Without any real proof, the police developed a theory that, before the robbery, the bandits had stored the Buick in a shed next to a second car owned by a man of Italian ancestry. After the Italian man took the second car to a garage for repairs, the police staked out the place. Confused statements from witnesses and a handful of spent shells were the only clues authorities had when they arrested Nicola Sacco and Bartolomeo Vanzetti on the night of May 5th, just because they accompanied the Italian man to pick up his car at the repair shop.

Back in the 1920s, ballistics tests couldn't match bullets to individual guns, so the pistols the defendants were caught with didn't really prove very much. In spite of skimpy evidence, though, the district attorney forged ahead with a six-week trial that only drew small crowds. The notorious case of Sacco and Vanzetti didn't capture the public's attention until a Dedham jury found both defendants guilty of murder in the first degree.

Sacco and Vanzetti were both Italian immigrants as well as active anarchists who believed in using violence to overthrow the government. At the very end of World War I and the start of the communist threat, it was a bad time in America to speak with a foreign accent or express unpopular views. When the defendants hired a West Coast lawyer connected to their radical cause to defend them, battle lines were drawn that touched off a fierce debate.

Did political and ethnic prejudice lead to a "legal lynching" and frame two innocent men for a crime they didn't commit? Or were Sacco and Vanzetti just sleazy bandits who murdered in cold blood and got what they deserved?

By the fall of 1921, people had begun to protest the conviction of Sacco and Vanzetti. But as their appeal dragged on for nearly five years, interest in the case waned and the future of the defendants looked increasingly dark. Most people seemed to agree with the Massachusetts court—if innocent men were executed, justice was still served as long as their trial was fair.

Early in 1927, after all appeals had failed, Felix Frankfurter, a former federal official and influential Professor of Law at Harvard University, pointed out that government witnesses could not identify Nicola Sacco until after they were coached. In his book, *The Case of Sacco and Vanzetti*, he wrote that thirty-one witnesses testified that Bartolomeo Vanzetti was not in the getaway car and that thirteen more people swore that they saw him selling fish on the day the robbery occurred. Frankfurter also explained how the judge and district attorney had inflamed the jury with the defendant's political views. He said that the judge had instructed the jury that a bullet in Berardelli's body was fired from Sacco's pistol when, in fact, the testimony was only that it came from a similar gun. Frankfurter even said that another criminal had confessed to the brutal crime and showed in painful detail how the legal system had failed.

When Frankfurter's book was released, the passions of the public were wildly stirred. Liberal writers and academics rallied to the cause and demonstrated in the streets of Boston. Protestors and policemen fell into an odd routine as demonstrators were led away and arrested again and again. Petitions with over 600,000 signatures demanding a new trial were delivered to the State House in Boston as people gathered from around the world to express their outraged views. But the wheels of justice in Massachusetts had ground to a stubborn halt. The date for the executions neared.

As the clock ticked toward midnight on August 23, 1927, a silent mob of citizens assembled in a large square outside the Charlestown Prison. Horses reared and flashed their hooves above the heads of the crowd as mounted policemen galloped about to maintain control. Anxious people milled in the streets to protest not only the approaching deaths but also a legal system that couldn't admit that it might be wrong. At midnight, lights in the prison tower blinked on and off and the large crowd went home. Sacco and Vanzetti were dead.

On the fiftieth anniversary of the executions, Michael Dukakis, Governor of Massachusetts, proclaimed a memorial day for Nicola Sacco and Bartolomeo Vanzetti. His declaration asked that all stigma be forever removed from their names and urged the citizens of Massachusetts to "prevent the forces of intolerance, fear, and hatred from ever again uniting to overcome the rationality, wisdom, and fairness to which our legal system aspires." The entire resolution should be read carefully, though. It never claims they weren't guilty. The case of Sacco and Vanzetti remains unsolved.

CHAPTER TWENTY-FIVE

Building a Berkshire Shed
·1938·

If the rich and famous wanted to enjoy the seaside early in the twentieth century, they flocked to palatial mansions in Newport, Rhode Island. If mountains were preferred, they turned to majestic summer homes in the beautiful Berkshire hills near Lenox, Massachusetts.

A refuge for the upper class, the Berkshires also served as the inspiration for a variety of well-known artists. Writers like Herman Melville, Nathaniel Hawthorne, and Oliver Wendell Holmes retreated to this scenic region populated by wealthy families like the Vanderbilts and Carnegies. In keeping with local customs that mingled wealth and culture, Gertrude Robinson Smith, a no-nonsense socialite who summered in a Berkshire cottage, gathered a few of her summer friends at the height of the Great Depression and organized the first festival of symphonic music to echo in the Berkshire hills.

With sixty-five members of the New York Philharmonic Symphony Orchestra borrowed for the weekend, the first Berkshire Symphonic Festival was held in the open air in 1934. After members of high society parked their cars in a pasture, they settled onto wooden benches set up in a horse corral and listened to classical music under a full August moon. The three-concert series was considered a great success and a grand excuse to rejuvenate the Berkshire social scene. Lawn parties and formal dinners preceded the event that attracted five thousand people dressed in elegant clothes and decked with expensive jewels. Luckily for all who attended, the weather remained fair.

The following year, twenty musicians were added to the makeshift orchestra, and the three-day event drew even larger crowds to the outdoor horse corral. Already, though, their instant success allowed trustees of the festival to dream of hiring a permanent orchestra to provide programs of the highest quality year after year. Their dreams were soon fulfilled. When world-renowned Russian conductor Serge Koussevitzky and the Boston Symphony Orchestra agreed to play the summer series in 1936, the Berkshire Music Festival immediately seized a prominent spot on the national music scene and secured a bright future. But the elegant Russian maestro wouldn't work in the open air. He insisted on one condition. Every concert he conducted had to be held under cover.

Koussevitzky and trustees of the festival searched for a suitable home for their world-class musicians until Mrs. Gorham Brooks and Miss Mary Aspinwall Tappan simply offered to give the Boston Symphony Orchestra a 210-acre estate just three miles away from the horse corral where the festival was first held. Named Tanglewood by Nathaniel Hawthorne while he lived and worked on the grounds, the Tappan family estate became the permanent home of the Berkshire Music Festival and the permanent summer residence of the Boston Symphony Orchestra. Overlooking Lake Mahkeenac, Monument Mountain, and the beautiful Berkshire hills, the sweeping lawns of this grand Victorian manor were the perfect site for a festival that had gained a brilliant reputation. The first concert at Tanglewood was held under a circus tent on the grand lawn on Thursday evening August 12, 1937.

Gathered for a rousing concert of the music of Richard Wagner, a typically stylish Berkshire crowd heard the rolling rumble of thunder intrude on the opening chords. Five thousand people stayed in their seats as a powerful summer storm pummeled the Tanglewood grounds. Umbrellas sprouted up throughout the crowd as thunder boomed, lightning cracked, and a flood of torrential rain drenched the leaky circus tent. Koussevitzky halted the orchestra three separate times and, in the end, the musical program had to be shortened. Surprisingly, though, the thunderstorm was hardly a disaster. What better way to convince a well-dressed crowd of the need for a music pavilion than to soak them with water? Before the end of the intermission on that rain-drenched summer night, Gertrude Robinson Smith had raised a third of the money needed to build a weatherproof concert hall.

Built with a 350-foot-long curved side that opens onto a broad lawn, Tanglewood's music pavilion now covers more than one and a half acres and seats more than five thousand people. The fan-shaped building was designed by the famous architect Eliel Saarinen, but the actual building he designed would have cost more than the budget allowed. When his plans were revised by Joseph Franz, a local engineer, Saarinen refused to have his name associated with the cheaper building. The festival, he complained, shouldn't have hired an architect if it only wanted a shed. Inaugurated on August 5, 1938, the Music Shed still stands as the focal point of Berkshire summer music.

Rededicated as the Koussevitzky Music Shed on its fiftieth anniversary in 1988, Tanglewood's famed pavilion has seen many changes on the growing festival grounds. Seiji Ozawa Hall (a center for chamber music), a small theater (for opera), and the Tanglewood Music Center (a prestigious summer academy for young musicians of promise) now share an expanded campus. Gone is the festival dress code that forced women to wear skirts. People in shorts and sandals now roam the Tanglewood lawn, and contemporary music is even allowed on the program. Yet in spite of change and improvement, the wooden roof and steel girders of Tanglewood's famous shed still project a marvelous sound. Thousands of lovers of classical music and fresh country air still converge in July and August to picnic on the tree-lined lawn while music drifts from the music shed to enliven the Berkshire hills.

CHAPTER TWENTY-SIX

The Microwave Revolution
· 1945 ·

W hen atom bombs fell on Hiroshima and Nagasaki and ended World War II, the eyes of the world focused on the brilliant physicists who created the deadly bombs and started the nuclear age. Overlooked by the admiring public, though, was another group of scientists who had worked year after year to create a series of high-tech devices that were the real winners of the war.

Before a plane with atomic bombs could fly over Japan, the Allies needed to stop the missiles that were raining down on London, turn the tide against German U-boats sinking ships in the North Atlantic, and push the powerful Japanese Navy back across the Pacific Ocean. Revolutionary at the time, the same forces that now carry e-mail and cook our frozen dinners made each of these things possible. In a crash program of innovation in Massachusetts, brilliant minds perfected microwave radar and designed guidance and detection systems that changed the course of the war.

Searching for elusive "death rays" (some kind of radiation that would kill enemy soldiers like a weapon in a science fiction book), Britain, Germany, Japan, and the United States had only crude knowledge of radar when World War II began. Limited to line of sight and only accurate to a thousand feet, the infant British radar system proved useful in 1940 when it spotted waves of German aircraft that attacked during the day. At that time, guidance systems that could track planes attacking at night, pinpoint incoming missiles, or spot a lurking periscope in the sweep of a choppy sea were far beyond everyone's wildest dreams.

Pursuing the "practical application of science" since 1861, the Massachusetts Institute of Technology (MIT) had earned a worldwide reputation as a high-tech center of knowledge. Urgently needing technical help to resist German bombing, the British carried their latest inventions to a crude Radiation Laboratory (Rad Lab) that had been hastily assembled at MIT near the banks of the Charles River in Cambridge, Massachusetts. Supplied with a new British gadget that generated microwaves (short wavelength bursts of electromagnetic energy), brilliant young scientists gathered from across the United States to rise to the challenge. As the roof of the nondescript Rad Lab sprouted large antennas and an odd assortment of boxes, the scientists trained their experimental radar units on the skyline of downtown Boston rather than German aircraft, and fishing trawlers off Cape Cod unwittingly acted as substitute targets for lurking submarines.

By November 1940, scientists at the Rad Lab had cobbled together a microwave radar as big as the building's roof, designed a smaller model that fit in a military plane, and successfully performed air-to-air and air-to-surface radar detection of aircraft and submarines.

In the five years of its existence, the Rad Lab grew from a core of twenty scientists who knew almost nothing about microwave radar to a staff of nearly four thousand who were experts in the radar field. Professionals associated with the Rad Lab extended their knowledge after the war and went on to harvest ten Nobel Prizes in specialties that ranged from astronomy to the mysteries of quantum physics.

Teaming up with companies such as Raytheon, Bell Laboratories, and scores of civilian industries that manufactured military hardware, the Rad Lab developed several ingenious devices.

Accelerating progress to an unimagined pace, the Rad Lab perfected gunlaying radar that locked onto targets and triggered accurate fire; navigational systems that guided allied aircraft to targets in any weather; landing systems that allowed aircraft to return safely home; systems that permitted precision bombing of obscure enemy targets; Microwave Early Warning systems (MEWs) that intercepted enemy missiles 130 miles away; radar based artillery fuses that sensed approaching targets; and even a radar based altitude fuse that triggered the atomic bomb.

While military systems moved from theory to mass production in record time during World War II, decades would pass before the world would reap all of the benefits of the Rad Lab's advances. From microwave ovens to wireless communications, from speed guns to radar antennas that explore interstellar space, a host of innovations that define the modern age trace their roots to the microwave research that flourished during World War II in the Rad Lab at MIT.

CHAPTER TWENTY-SEVEN

The Cocoanut Grove Fire
• 1942 •

Remember those old black and white movies Hollywood made in the big-band era? Set in sophisticated nightclubs where chorus girls and a slinky singer put on a brassy show, the films portrayed supper clubs where champagne flowed freely and the good times rolled. In these swanky movie nightspots, men in tuxedos and gorgeous women surveyed a stylish dance floor from choice balcony tables high above the scene, and powerful people partied with patrons with naughty reputations.

The hugely popular Cocoanut Grove, near the theater district in Boston, lived up to this Hollywood image. On Saturday night, November 28, 1942, extra tables edged onto the Grove's dance floor to accommodate the large crowd, while down in the basement many couples gathered around the oval bar in the intimate Melody Lounge. Beneath a ceiling of billowing folds of blue satin sky, artificial palm fronds fluttered overhead, plenty of bamboo and rattan set a tropical tone, and customers sprawled in total comfort on fake leather chairs.

All that changed just after 10:00 P.M. that cold, autumn night. Blazing out of the darkness of the crowded Melody Lounge, a raging inferno swept the Grove with unbelievable speed. From the first glimmering spark of fire to the last death that it caused, just twelve minutes went by.

Officially, the source of the fire has never been determined. Investigators found a faulty wire that may have caused the blaze, but patrons saw a bus boy strike a match as he tried to replace a light bulb in the corner of the basement bar. A few seconds after the match was struck, a spark fluttered on a waving frond and a growing circle of fire ignited the billowing decorations.

The blowtorch that hit the Cocoanut Grove was no everyday fire. As the fake leather and dry decorations continued to smolder and spark, bar customers passed out from the noxious fumes before they could rise from their seats. Hot gases and poisonous smoke turned the stairway into a chimney. Patrons who ran for the exit lost their race to safety when a ball of super-hot gas found a supply of oxygen and exploded at the top of the stairs. In the first minutes of the fire, people died in the basement where screaming hysteria reigned, while customers on the floor above continued to dance, unaware of the fire below.

After black smoke and hot gas blasted up the stairs and charged the front foyer, the inferno raced the length of the entrance hall in only a few seconds. Pushed along by a fan that was meant to cool the dining area, half-burned compressed gas invaded the Cocoanut Grove's main room and literally torched the club. The fire spread so fast that the Grove became a gutted shell in less than five minutes.

Death converged at the exits. Throats seared, hair singed, lungs clogged with smoke, panicked customers rushed for the same outlets that the lethal gases used. An emergency exit had been welded shut to keep intruders out, and patrons trying to flee the building through another door could not get it open because of all the people pushing against them. The patrons had nowhere to go and as they gathered together in a desperate mass, they were blasted with burning gases that rolled off the ceiling. Asphyxiated or scorched by flame, scores of people fell dead in front of the exits creating a gruesome human barrier that cut off all escape. As they urgently tried to find survivors and douse the roaring flames, firemen actually burned their hands removing the piled bodies.

Many stories of escape and rescue grew out of that night at the Cocoanut Grove. A bartender grabbed a towel along with a pitcher of water, made a mask, and sat on the floor until the fumes lifted. A few people survived by getting in a walk-in cooler just off the downstairs kitchen. A bus boy stuck his head in a half-empty ice cream drum and cheated the grim reaper. The people of Boston responded readily to the disaster by carrying victims away from the burned building or by giving blood to help the wounded. Boston cabs were used as hearses to carry charred bodies to the morgue.

Even a few good things came out of the Cocoanut Grove Fire. Advances in treating burn victims were perfected in the months that followed, and to this day, the tragedy at the Cocoanut Grove is cited as the reason that fire codes now prohibit such flammable materials as decorations in public buildings and also require sprinklers, emergency lighting, and exit doors that open out.

CHAPTER TWENTY-EIGHT

The Brinks Job
· 1950 ·

The crooks knew the routine. Every day as businesses closed throughout Boston, armored cars rolled into the city's North End with payroll checks, negotiable bonds, and bulging bags of cash. Headed for a plain, three-story building between Prince and Hull Streets, the treasure was off to be counted at the headquarters of Brinks Inc. Laundry hampers full of loot streamed into the money room so quickly that the Brinks vault was left open for two hours every night while tellers finished the count.

A rogue's gallery of all-stars from the Boston underworld spent months casing the joint. The South End gang crept into the building thirty times to learn its every nook and cranny. Night after night, they stole the knobs off doors, cut duplicate keys, and replaced the pilfered locks. With a lookout posted on top of a tenement located across the street, the gang knew when police patrolled, when guards came and went, and when office workers in the Brinks building retired for the night.

The thieves thought of everything. They even staged a dress rehearsal of their planned robbery. After four or five false starts when conditions weren't quite right, seven men of medium height, all dressed in navy pea coats and caps with green visors, walked into the Brinks stronghold as if they owned the place. With drill team precision, they donned gargoyle masks, snuck up the stairs, and headed for the vault. Armed with stolen guns, they got the drop on the tellers and guards, tied them with ropes and tape, and made off with more cash than any crook had ever seen. The heist lasted seventeen minutes, and the thieves got away with three million dollars. It was almost the perfect crime.

Even after fleeing the scene in a stolen truck, the thugs were very careful. They burned nearly one hundred thousand dollars in new currency and a million dollars in bonds which they knew the cops could trace. They threw their guns in the river, burned the disguises they had worn, and even cut the stolen getaway truck up into small pieces and left the pieces in Stoughton's town dump.

With no signs of a break-in, the FBI and Boston Police figured it was an inside job, but they rounded up the usual suspects and followed a thousand leads. A gun turned up. Pieces of the truck were found. But the only evidence from the crime scene was a cap they couldn't trace. Because all the thieves looked alike, eyewitness accounts were useless. The tellers and guards couldn't even tell how many crooks were involved in the robbery.

Meanwhile, the members of the South End gang acted like nothing had happened. The lookout, Vinnie Costa, the driver, Joe Banfield, and the crooks, "Specs" O'Keefe, Tony Pino, "Jazz" Maffie, Mike Geagan, "Gus" Gusciora, Henry Baker, James Faherty, and Thomas Richardson all trusted Joe McGinnis. McGinnis was the brains of the operation, but he didn't go anywhere near the Brinks building and had an alibi. McGinnis took most of the money "to keep it safe" until the ruckus died.

Crooks are crooks and greed is greed, and they're hard to separate. The cops had no evidence, just pretty strong suspicions. They put a tail on "Specs" O'Keefe and "Gus" Gusciora.

Trouble started when "Specs" and "Gus" were jailed in Pennsylvania for unrelated crimes, and none of their buddies helped them out. They sent messages and passed the word, but they got no bail, no money for lawyers, and no cash to pay guys off. Their friends let them rot in prison for months, and "Specs" O'Keefe let the gang know he was not a happy man.

When "Specs" got out of jail, he went looking for explanations—and his share of the stolen cash. What he got instead was a gunfight, a drive-by shooting, and a hit man from New York who blasted him with machine gun fire as he walked down a street in Boston. Luckily for "Specs," "Trigger" Burke was a lousy shot.

Wounded in the wrist and chest, fearing for his life, and still facing more criminal charges in the state of Pennsylvania, "Specs" O'Keefe had only one way to turn. Just five days before a statute of limitations would prevent prosecutions for any role in the Brinks Job, "Specs" O'Keefe and the district attorney agreed to cut a deal.

O'Keefe testified at the trial of the South End gang. The members of the gang were sentenced to life in prison. McGinnis and Baker died in prison, but the others eventually made parole. After the trial, "Specs" O'Keefe went to California, adopted a new name, and started a new life.

What happened to the money? Joe McGinnis probably knew. Of the millions of dollars that were stolen, less than one hundred thousand dollars was ever found.

CHAPTER TWENTY-NINE

A Special Birthday Salute
· 1976 ·

Exactly two hundred years after the Declaration of Independence was adopted on July 4, 1776, the nation threw a party. From coast to coast, fireworks and grand parades marked the bicentennial. Ten thousand people marched in the nation's capital, millions watched a flotilla of ships sail into New York Harbor, and a chorus of bells from across the land answered the ring of the Liberty Bell from Independence Hall in Philadelphia.

But while other towns celebrated with patriotic enthusiasm, none could match the sense of living history that energized the city where the fight for freedom began. Harkening back to its glory days when square-rigged sailing ships floated in its harbor and the city began to call itself the Hub of the Universe, Boston celebrated July 4, 1976, with a special flare that proclaimed the city's historic pride and honored the nation's birth.

Mayor Kevin White raised the stars and stripes downtown at City Hall as muskets fired, bands played, and thousands of people waved their own miniature American flags. Thousands sang the National Anthem in a packed Faneuil Hall, and wreaths were laid at the graves of Samuel Adams, John Hancock, and Robert Trent Paine (three signers of the Declaration of Independence) in the Old Granary Burying Ground in the central business district.

In the afternoon, fifty thousand citizens gathered on the grassy esplanade along the banks of the Charles River in eager anticipation of the evening's crowning event. By nightfall, a throng of 400,000 rejoiced with wild applause as Arthur Fiedler, conductor of the Boston Pops, struck up the "Star Spangled Banner." A national television audience thrilled to a Boston tradition as the Boston Pops Orchestra climaxed the night of celebration with the stirring strains of the "1812 Overture" punctuated by fireworks and the explosion of 1,200 aerial shells that brightened the Boston sky.

The highlight of Boston's celebration of the nation's bicentennial occurred one week after July 4th when the USS *Constitution* nudged away from its berth at the Charlestown Navy Yard. Commissioned by the U.S. Congress in 1794 and built in East Boston in 1797, the USS *Constitution* is the world's oldest commissioned warship and the winner of more than forty historic naval battles. Nicknamed *Old Ironsides* when shells from the British frigate *Guerriere* bounced off its wooden hull during the War of 1812, this proud Navy warship hadn't gone to sea or fired its massive cannons for nearly one hundred years.

Newly refurbished for the bicentennial celebration, *Old Ironsides* was propelled by tugs to the entrance to Boston Harbor. Resplendent with pitch pine planking, black oak bow, and three towering masts up to 187 feet high, *Old Ironsides* was greeted by a glorious parade of historic sailing ships. Sixty-six vessels from more than a dozen nations together with a handful of Tall Ships, each more than two hundred feet long, gathered off Deer Island for a six-mile parade into Boston's inner harbor. Led by the USS

Constitution, an armada of schooners, ketches, sloops, yawls, barks, and brigantines delighted 650,000 spectators who lined the shores of South Boston, watched from more than 3,600 pleasure boats that crowded into the harbor, or partied in downtown office towers that flanked the waterfront.

With sails unfurled, the marine parade eased into Boston Harbor with a gentle wind from the stern. Fireboats shot watery plumes into the summer sky. Nautical bells and horns sounded in noisy celebration. But the loudest and proudest salute of the day came from the oldest source. Silent since 1880, two 6,300-pound cast-iron cannons mounted in *Old Ironsides'* bow roared a tribute once a minute for a full hour and a half as the line of majestic sailing ships proudly turned at India Wharf and docked at a Boston pier. On that day in 1976, the masts and riggings of sailing ships and the USS *Constitution* brought the sights and sounds of 1776 to Boston's inner harbor in reminder of the patriots who once hosted a tea party and began the struggle for independence.

CHAPTER THIRTY

Johnny Kelley's 60th Boston Marathon
· 1991 ·

T he Boston Marathon is the oldest foot race in America and still the most revered. First run in 1897 by fifteen men who wore heavy boots and trudged over dirt roads, this annual Patriot's Day race from Hopkinton to Boston attracted more than thirty-eight thousand contestants to its recent centennial run.

The folklore of the Boston Marathon adds to its mystique. In the early days, people who ran the 26 miles 285 yards were considered slightly odd. Colorful winners like Clarence H. DeMar (a seven-time champ), Ellison "Tarzan" Brown (a Narragansett Indian), and Gerard Cote (a cigar-smoking Quebecois) all left their indelible marks on the race before the end of World War II.

As local fans know, the Boston Marathon has always stressed participation rather than winning and losing. A blind person ran the race in 1975, and in the 1990s, one man ran facing backwards over the entire length of the course, and a police officer ran while pushing a wheelchair that held his disabled son. Thousands of people start the Boston race just to be part of a famed event. The challenge, however, is to finish. Long after the top contenders have showered and gone home, fans in Boston still applaud the plodders who struggle across the finish line with the pride of a personal victory.

Nothing has better captured the spirit of the Boston Marathon than the run of Johnny A. Kelley in 1991. Flanked by two honor guards from the Massachusetts State Police, this five-foot six-inch, eighty-three-year-old Irishman with green eyes and spindly legs chugged along on his sixtieth Boston Marathon start. True to Boston tradition, fans still rooted for Johnny even though he was not among the winners of the race.

Johnny Kelley first ran in the Boston Marathon in 1928 when he was twenty years old. He didn't make it to the finish line that first year nor did he make it in 1932 when he tried the race again. Johnny didn't give up, though. Year after year, he continued to participate in the marathon, and in 1935, he won. He won again ten years later at the age of thirty-seven. He finished second seven times, had nineteen top ten finishes, and crossed the line in the top twenty an astonishing twenty-five times. He dropped out of the race in 1956 because he had the flu, but over the next thirty-five years, Johnny A. Kelley made certain that he finished every Boston race he started.

Johnny managed to place second in the Boston Marathon in 1943 while he was a soldier in the U.S. Army. In 1948, Johnny won the AAU National Marathon Championship at the age of forty-one and earned an award as the AAU New England Athlete of the Year eighteen years later at the age of fifty-nine!

As the years went by, Johnny's pace slowed but knowledgeable fans understood that winning was no longer what Johnny desired. Year after year, Johnny Kelley ended the Boston Marathon by waving to his fans and blowing kisses to the girls.

Spectators knew that the marathon wasn't over until Johnny crossed the finish line. And so it was in 1991. When Johnny crossed the finish line in the rain at the end of his sixtieth run, press photographers, race officials, and cheering fans greeted him as he ran into Boston history and broke a commemorative tape that honored an inspiring lifetime of marathon achievement.

CHAPTER THIRTY-ONE

A Potpourri of Massachusetts Facts

• Massachusetts is the forty-fourth largest state in the nation with a total area of 10,554.79 square miles. Of that total, 2,716.81 square miles are covered by water.

• Mount Greylock, in the northwest corner of the state, is the highest point in Massachusetts at an altitude of 3,491 feet. Designed as a lighthouse, the War Memorial Tower is located at the top of Mount Greylock and allows visitors to climb another one hundred feet above the open summit.

• The geographical center of Massachusetts is located in the southern part of the city of Worcester.

• Massachusetts has fourteen counties.

• The capital of Massachusetts is Boston.

• The largest city in Massachusetts is Boston. In 1994, Boston had a population of 547,725.

• The 1990 Census concluded that Massachusetts had a population of 6,073,550, making Massachusetts the thirteenth most populated state in the nation.

• Massachusetts was the sixth colony to join the United States on February 6, 1788.

• The Massachusetts state constitution was adopted in 1780 making it the oldest state constitution still in effect in the United States.

• Massachusetts contains more than 285,000 acres of state forests and parks. Its largest state forest is the 16,127-acre October Mountain State Forest in Lee. Its smallest state park is the one-acre City Square Park in Charlestown.

• Lake Chargoggagoggmanchauggagoggchaubunagungamaugg is located in the town of Webster, Massachusetts. The name is the longest for any lake in the United States.

• From Provincetown to Chatham, forty miles of beaches are preserved in the Cape Cod National Seashore.

• The hottest temperature ever recorded in Massachusetts was 107 degrees Fahrenheit and was recorded at both Chester and New Bedford on August 2, 1975.

• The coldest temperature ever recorded in Massachusetts was thirty-five degrees below zero which was recorded in the town of Chester on January 12, 1981.

• Massachusetts is nicknamed the Bay State.

• The official state flower is the mayflower, and the state tree is the American elm.

• The state bird is the chickadee, and the state insect is the ladybug.

• The official state beverage is cranberry juice, the state muffin is made of corn, and the official state dessert is, of course, Boston cream pie.

Further Reading

Benzaquin, Paul. *Holocaust.* New York: Holt, 1959.

Boettinger, H. M. *The Telephone Book: Bell, Watson, Vail, and American Life, 1876-1976.* New York: Riverwood, 1977.

Buderi, Robert. *The Invention That Changed the World: How a Small Group of Radar Pioneers Won the Second World War and Launched a Technological Revolution.* New York: Simon & Schuster, 1996.

Cable, Mary. *The Blizzard of '88.* New York: Atheneum, 1988.

Calloway, Colin, ed. *Dawnland Encounters: Indians and Europeans in Northern New England.* Hanover, NH: University Press of New England, 1991.

Falls, Joe. *The Boston Marathon.* New York: Macmillan, 1977.

Fischer, David H. *Paul Revere's Ride.* New York: Oxford University Press, 1994.

Frankfurter, Felix. *The Case of Sacco and Vanzetti.* New York: Universal Library, 1927.

Howe, Donald W. *Quabbin: The Lost Valley.* Salem, MA: Higginson Book Co., 1992.

Kent, David. *Forty Whacks: New Evidence in the Life and Legend of Lizzie Borden.* Emmaus, PA: Yankee Books, 1992.

Kupferberg, Herbert. *Tanglewood.* New York: McGraw-Hill, 1976.

Labaree, Benjamin Woods. *The Boston Tea Party.* New York: Oxford University Press, 1964.

Lepore, Jill. *The Name of War.* New York: Alfred A. Knopf, 1998.

Levin, David. *What Happened in Salem? Documents Pertaining to the Seventeenth-Century Witchcraft Trials.* New York: Harcourt, Brace, 1960.

Lewis, Frederick, and Dick Johnson. *Young at Heart: Johnny Kelley.* Waco, TX: WRS Publishing, 1992.

Melville, Herman. *Moby Dick.* New York: Barnes & Noble Books, 1993.

O'Keefe, Joseph James. *The Men Who Robbed Brinks.* New York: Random House, 1961.

Pincus, Andrew. *Scenes From Tanglewood.* Boston: Northeastern University Press, 1989.

Russell, Francis. *A City in Terror: 1919, the Boston Police Strike.* New York: Viking Press, 1975.

Shanks, Ralph, et. al. *U.S. Life-Saving Service: Heroes, Rescues, and Architecture of the Early Coast Guard.* Pestaluna, CA: Costano Books, 1996.

Spiering, Frank. *Lizzie.* New York: Random House, 1984.

Starkey, Marion L. *A Little Rebellion.* New York: Alfred A. Knopf, 1955.

————. *The Devil in Massachusetts: A Modern Inquiry into the Salem Witch Trials.* New York: Alfred A. Knopf, 1949.

Szatmary, David. *Shay's Rebellion.* Amherst: University of Massachusetts Press, 1980.

Thoreau, Henry David. *Walden.* Cutchogue, NY: Buccaneer Books, 1986.

Vaughan, Alden T. *New England Frontier: Puritans and Indians 1620– 1675.* New York: W.W. Norton & Co., 1979.

Webb, Bernice L. *The Basketball Man, James Naismith.* Lawrence: University Press of Kansas, 1973.

Young, William, and David Kaiser. *Postmortem: New Evidence in the Case of Sacco and Vanzetti.* Amherst: University of Massachusetts Press, 1985.

Index